# *When Someone Dies*
## IN ILLINOIS

ALL THE LEGAL AND PRACTICAL THINGS
YOU NEED TO DO
WHEN SOMEONE NEAR TO YOU DIES
IN THE STATE OF ILLINOIS

By AMELIA E. POHL, Attorney at Law
with
CHESTER M. PRZYBYLO as consulting
Attorney at Law for Illinois law
and
BARBARA J. SIMMONDS, Ph.D.
as consulting psychologist

 EAGLE PUBLISHING COMPANY OF BOCA

The purpose of this book is to provide the reader with an accurate and informative overview of the subject but laws change frequently and are subject to different interpretations as courts rule on the meaning or effect of a law. This book is sold with the understanding that neither the publisher nor the authors are engaging in, nor rendering legal, medical, psychiatric, accounting or any other professional service. If you need legal, accounting, medical, psychiatric or other expert advice, then you should seek the services of a duly licensed professional.

WEB SITES: Web sites appear throughout the book. These Web sites are offered for the convenience of the reader only. Publication of these Web site addresses is not an endorsement by the authors, editors or publishers of this book.

This book is intended for use by the consumer for his or her own benefit. If you use this book to counsel someone about the law, accounting or medicine, then that may be considered an unauthorized and illegal practice.

EAGLE PUBLISHING COMPANY OF BOCA
4199 N. Dixie Highway, #2
Boca Raton, FL    33431
E-mail   info@eaglepublishing.com

Printed in the United States of America
ISBN 1-892407-11-6  CASE BOUND
ISBN 1-892407-12-4  PERFECT BOUND
Library of Congress Card Catalog Number: 99-69964

# About the Author

Before becoming an attorney in 1985, AMELIA E. POHL taught mathematics on both the high school and college level. During her tenure as Associate Professor of Mathematics at Prince George's Community College in Maryland, she wrote several books including Probability: A Set Theory Approach, Principals of Counting and Common Stock Sense.

During her practice of law Attorney Pohl observed that many people want to reduce the high cost of legal fees by performing or assisting with their own legal transactions. Attorney Pohl found that, with a bit of guidance, people are able to perform many legal transactions for themselves. Attorney Pohl is utilizing her background as teacher, author and attorney to provide that "bit of guidance" to the general public in the form of self-help legal books that she has written. Attorney Pohl is currently working on "translating" this book for the rest of the 49 states:

*When Someone Dies In Alabama,*

*When Someone Dies in Connecticut,* etc.

CHESTER M. PRZYBYLO, a Georgetown University graduate, earned an MBA in finance from the University of Chicago, and his Juris Doctorate from ITT Chicago-Kent College of Law. Mr. Przybylo is recognized for his expertise in planning estates to reduce taxes, preserve assets and avoid probate. He is a widely-known and sought-after speaker who has educated thousands of individuals on these subjects. Practicing for over 30 years, he has developed imaginative and creative estate planning strategies based on solid legal and tax principals and is called upon frequently for planning strategies.

A partner in the law firm of Przybylo, Kubiatowski, and Associates, Mr. Przybylo has been meeting the needs of Chicago area clients since 1968. His practice focuses on estate and business planning, living trusts, wills probate, elder law and asset protection. Whether a client's estate is small, modest or considerable, Mr. Przybylo finds it very satisfying to tailor an estate plan to suit the client's personal needs.

Mr. Przybylo is a pioneer in educating the public on proper estate planning. He is a founding member of the National Network of Estate Planning Attorneys, a charter member of the American Academy of Estate Planning Attorneys, a charter member of the American Academy of Estate Planning Attorneys and the American Institute of Estate Planning Attorneys. He is a member of the Chicago Bar Association, the Chicago Estate Planning Council and the American Bar Association.

In addition to his speaking engagements, busy practice and contributing to this book as consulting counsel for Illinois law, Mr. Przybylo has co-authored four books:
- ✍ Legacy: Plan, Protect and Preserve Your Estate
- ✍ Ways and Means: Maximize the Value
       of Your Retirement Savings
- ✍ Generations
- ✍ Strictly Business

# *Consulting Psychologist*

BARBARA J. SIMMONDS, Ph.D., a noted psychologist, has collaborated with the author on those sections of this book dealing with the grieving process. Dr. Simmonds has been practicing in the field of Health/Rehabilitation Psychology and Gerontology for the past 10 years. Her experiences in the field led her as a natural outcome to develop expertise also in Grief Counseling, since so many losses accrue to individuals in a health care setting.

In addition to her work in hospitals, nursing centers and private practice, Dr. Simmonds has served as Adjunct Faculty at Nova Southeastern University, teaching courses in Aging, Stress Management and Grief Counseling. Dr. Simmonds holds a Master's Degree in Gerontology and a Ph.D. in Clinical Psychology from Nova Southeastern University. She was the Director of Psychological Services at Villa Maria Nursing and Rehabilitation Center for eight years and now continues her relationship with the institution on a consultation basis. She continues with her private practice in North Miami, Florida.

# ACKNOWLEDGMENTS

When someone dies, the family attorney is often among the first to be called. Family members have questions about whether probate is necessary, who to notify, how to get possession of the assets, etc. Over the years, as we practiced in the field of Elder Law, we noticed that the questions raised were much the same family to family. We both agreed that a book answering such questions would be of service to the general public. We wish to thank all of the clients, whom we have had the honor and pleasure to serve, for providing us with the impetus to produce this book.

Special thanks from AMELIA E. POHL
I wish to express my sincere appreciation for the assistance and encouragement given to me by Michael J. DeMarie, CPA, my assistant Martha Dermer, my brother Paul Adinolfi, my daughters Louise Lucas and Margot Bosche, and to my husband J. William Pohl.

Special thanks from CHESTER M. PRZYBYLO
No one can complete his or her life-long mission in a vacuum. I'd like to thank the guiding lights behind all the estate planning organizations that I've participated in founding, or of which I am a member. My special gratitude to my wife, Elizabeth R. Przybylo, for her support in all my endeavors.

# *When Someone Dies in Illinois*
## CONTENTS

# About this book

We have tried to make this book as comprehensive as possible so there are specialized sections of the book that do not apply to the general population and may not be of interest to you. The following GUIDE POSTS appear throughout the book. You can read the section if the situation applies to you or skip the section if it doesn't.

## GUIDE POSTS

The **SPOUSE POST** means that the information provided is specifically for the spouse of the decedent. If the decedent was single, then skip this section.

The **CALL-A-LAWYER POST** alerts you to a situation than may require the assistance of an attorney. See page xiii for information about how to find a lawyer.

The **SPECIAL SITUATION POST** means that the information given in that paragraph applies to a particular event or situation; for example when the decedent dies a violent death. If the situation does not apply in your case then you can skip the section.

The **CAUTION POST** alerts you to a potential problem. It is followed by a suggestion about how to avoid the problem.

# The Organization of the Book

There are six steps in settling the estate of the decedent:

1. Tending to the funeral and burial
2. Telling everyone that the person died
3. Locating all of the decedent's property
4. Paying any outstanding bills
5. Determining who are the beneficiaries
6. Getting the decedent's property to the proper beneficiary

We devoted a chapter to each of these 6 steps (see the table of contents). We placed a check list at the end of Chapter 6 as a summary of things that need to be done.

Chapters 1 through 6 identifies problems that can occur when someone dies. Chapters 7 and 8 explain how to set up your own estate plan so that your family is not burdened by similar problems.

Chapter 9 offers suggestions that may help if you are having difficulty getting through the grieving process.

## GLOSSARY

This book is designed for the average reader. Legal terminology has been kept to a minimum. There is a glossary at the end of the book in the event you come across a legal term that is not familiar to you.

## FICTITIOUS NAMES AND EVENTS

The examples in this book are based loosely on actual events; however, all names are fictitious and the events as portrayed, are fictitious.

## Reading the Law

Where applicable, we identified the state statute or federal statute that is the basis of the discussion. We did this as a reference, and also to encourage the general public to read the law as it is written. Prior to the Internet the only way you could look up the law was to physically take yourself to the local courthouse law library or the law section of a public library. Today all of the state and federal statutes are literally at your finger tips. They are just a mouse click away on the Internet. All you need to look up the law is the address of the web site and the identifying number of the statute:

ILLINOIS STATUTE WEB SITE
http://www.legis.state.il.us/

FEDERAL STATUTE WEB SITE
http://www4.law.cornell.edu/uscode

The Illinois legislature has compiled the Illinois statutes into 67 chapters. The chapters are numbered in multiples of 5:

Chapter 5: GENERAL PROVISIONS
Chapter 10: ELECTIONS
Chapter 15: EXECUTIVE OFFICERS, etc.

Each chapter is divided into Acts, and each Act is then divided into sections. The notation (225 ILCS 41/14-75) refers to:

Chapter 225 of the Illinois Compiled Statutes
Act 41 of Chapter 225
Section 14-75 of Act 41.

If you come across a topic that is of importance to you, then you may find it both interesting and profitable to actually read the law as written.

# When You Need A Lawyer

This book describes Illinois law as in effect when the book was written. We pay our legislators (state and federal) to make laws and, if necessary, change those in effect. We pay judges to interpret the law and that may change the way the law is put into effect. The legislature and the judiciary do their job and so laws are constantly changing.

The purpose of the book is to give the reader an overview of what needs to be done when someone dies, and to provide information about how a person can arrange his own affairs to avoid problems for his own family. It is not intended as a substitute for legal counsel or any other kind of professional advice. If you have any legal question, then you should seek the counsel of an attorney. When looking for an attorney, consider three things:

EXPERTISE, COST and PERSONALITY.

## EXPERTISE

The state of Illinois does not have a certification program so attorneys in that state may not hold themselves out as being a "certified specialist" in any given area of law. Attorneys are allowed to state that they concentrate on certain areas of law or that they limit their practice to an area of law. Before employing an attorney for a job, ask how long he has practiced that type of law and what percentage of his practice is devoted to that type of law.

The Illinois State Bar Association can refer you to an attorney for the type of legal service your need. You can call them at (800) 252-1760; or if you are calling from out of state call (217) 525-5297.

You can call any of the local Bar Association for a referral within that county. The number for the Chicago Bar Association is (312) 544-2001.

The Illinois Bar Association has a web site that gives the telephone numbers of the local Bar Associations:

 ILLINOIS STATE BAR ASSOCIATION WEB SITE
http://www.illinoisbar.org/

Of course, the best way to find an attorney, experienced in the type of law you seek, is through personal referral. Ask your friends, family or business acquaintances if they have used an attorney for the field of law that you seek and whether they were pleased with the results. It is important to employ an attorney who is experienced in the kind of law you seek. Your friend may have had a wonderful Estate Planning attorney, but if you have suffered an injury, then you need a Personal Injury attorney.

## COST

In addition to the attorney's experience, it is important that you check out what you can expect to pay in attorney's fees. When you call for an appointment ask what the attorney will charge for the initial consultation and the approximate cost for the service you seek. Ask whether there will be any additional costs such as filing fees, accounting fees, expert witness fees, etc.

If the least expensive attorney is out of your price range then there are many state and private agencies that provide legal assistance for people of low income, such as:

| | |
|---|---|
| Pro Bono Project of Will County | (815) 727-5123 |
| AIDS Legal Council of Chicago | (312) 427-8990 |
| West Central Illinois Legal Assistance | (309) 343-2141 |
| Prairie State Legal Services, Inc. | (309) 674-9831 |
| (Marshall, Peoria, Tazewell, Woodford counties) | |
| Prairie State Legal Services, Inc. | (815) 965-2902 |
| (Boone, Carroll, Ogle, Stephenson, Winnebago counties) | |
| Land of Lincoln Legal Assist. Foundation, Inc. | (800) 252-8629 |

You can call your local county Bar Association for a referral to the agency nearest you. The American Bar Association has a directory of local Pro Bono Programs at their Web Site:

 AMERICAN BAR ASSOCIATION
WEB SITE
http://www.abanet.org/legalservices/probono/pb-illinois.html

## PERSONALITY

Of equal importance to the attorney's experience and legal fees, is your relationship with the attorney. How easy was it to reach the attorney? Did you go through layers of receptionists and legal assistants before being allowed to speak to the attorney? Did the attorney promptly return your call? If you had difficulty reaching the attorney, then you can expect similar problems should you employ that attorney.

Did the attorney treat you with respect? Did the attorney treat you paternally with a "father knows best" attitude or did the attorney treat you as an intelligent person with the ability to understand the options available to you and the ability to make your own decision based on the information provided to you.

Are you able to understand and easily communicate with the attorney? Is he/she speaking to you in plain English or is his/her explanation of the matter so full of legalese to be almost meaningless to you?

Do you find the attorney's personality to be pleasant or grating? Sometimes people rub each other the wrong way. It is like rubbing a cat the wrong way. Stroking a cat from head to tail is pleasing to the cat, but petting it in the opposite direction, no matter how well intended, causes friction. If the lawyer makes you feel annoyed or uncomfortable then find another attorney.

It is worth the effort to take the time to interview as many attorneys as it takes to find one with the right expertise, fee schedule and personality for you.

# The First Week 1

Dealing with the death of a close family member or friend is difficult. Not only do you need to deal with your own emotions but often with those of your family and friends. In addition to the emotional impact of a death, there are many things that need to be done, from arranging the funeral and burial, to closing out the business affairs of the decedent, and finally giving whatever property is left to the proper beneficiary.

The funeral and burial take only a few days. Wrapping up the affairs of the decedent may take considerably longer. This chapter explains what things you (the spouse or closest family member) need to do during the first week, beginning at the moment of death and continuing through the funeral.

 MALE GENDER USED

Rather than use "he/she" or "his/her" for simplicity
(and hoping not to offend anyone)
we will refer to the decedent using the male gender.

References to other people will be in both genders.

# AUTOPSIES

Years ago people died natural deaths from unknown causes. Doctors often requested permission to perform an autopsy to determine the cause of death.  In today's high tech world of medicine, doctors are fairly certain of the cause of death, but if there is a question, the family may be asked permission to perform an autopsy. If, during his lifetime, the decedent signed a Power of Attorney for Health Care giving his Agent  authority to agree to an autopsy, then the Agent can consent to the autopsy.  If no Agent was appointed, then any relative who has the right to dispose of the body, may give consent.  If 2 or more people have equal rights to dispose of the body (for example, the decedent's  children, if he was not married) and one objects, in writing, to the physician performing the autopsy, then no autopsy can be performed (410 ILCS 505/2 a, b, d).

It may cost several hundred dollars to have an autopsy performed.  The person giving authorization must agree to pay for the autopsy because the cost is not covered under most health insurance plans.  It is in the family's best interest to consent to the autopsy because such examination might reveal a genetic disorder, that could be treated if it later appears in another family member. Even if no such disease is found, knowing the cause of death with certainty is better than not knowing.  An example that comes to mind is  a woman who was taken to the hospital complaining of stomach pains. The doctors thought she might be suffering from gallbladder disease but she died before they could  effectively treat her.  The doctor suggested that an autopsy be performed to  determine the actual cause of death.  The woman had three daughters, one of whom  objected to the autopsy:

"Why spend that kind of money?
It won't bring Mom back."

The daughter's wishes were respected, however over the years as each of the daughters aged and became ill with their own various ailments they would undergo physical examinations. As part of taking their medical history, doctors would routinely ask "And what was the cause of your mother's death?" None could answer the question.

This is not a dramatic story. No mysterious genetic disorder ever occurred in any of her children, nor in any of their children. But each daughter (including the one who objected) at some point in their life, was confronted with the nagging question "What did Mom die of?"

## MANDATORY AUTOPSIES

When a person dies, a physician must sign the death certificate stating the cause of death. If a person dies in a hospital, then there is a doctor present to sign the certificate. If a person dies at home from natural causes or any other reason (accident, violence, suicide) then the police must be notified. The person who discovers the body should call 911 to summon the police.

The police will ask the medical examiner or coroner to determine the causes of death. If there is a suspicion that the death was not from natural causes or if the decedent died from a disease that might pose a threat to the public health, then the coroner or medical examiner may order an autopsy. The cost of the autopsy is paid for from the general fund of the county where the body is found (55 ILCS 5/3-3014).

## AUTOPSIES PERFORMED BY THE INSURANCE COMPANY

Most accident and life insurance policies contain a provision that the company has the right to perform an autopsy. The cost of the autopsy is paid for by the insurance company, so they will not order an autopsy unless there is some important reason to do so.

# ANATOMICAL GIFTS

If, before death, the decedent made an anatomical gift by signing a donor card, then hospital personnel or the donor's doctor needs to be made aware of the gift in quick proximity to the time of death — preferably before death.

## GIFT AUTHORIZED BY THE FAMILY

Hospital personnel determine whether a mortally ill patient is a candidate for an organ donation. Early on in the donor program those over 65 were not considered as suitable candidates. Today, however, the condition of the organ, and not the age, is the determining factor.

The federal government has established regional Organ Procurement Organizations throughout the United States, to coordinate the donor program. The Organ Procurement Organization for the state of Illinois is called the Regional Organ Bank of Illinois, Inc. If it is decided that the patient is a candidate, the hospital will contact the Organ Bank.

The Organ Bank will determine whether the patient is a suitable donor. If they decide to request the gift and the candidate did not sign a donor card then someone must authorize the donation. Someone who is specially trained will approach the family to request the donation. If the decedent authorized such donation under a Power of Attorney for Health Care, then his Agent can agree authorize the gift, If not then Illinois statute (755 ILCS 50/3) establishes an order of priority to authorize the donation: 1st   The spouse

    2nd   An adult child of the decedent
    3rd   Either parent
    4th   An adult brother or sister
    5th   A guardian appointed prior to death
    6th   Anyone authorized to dispose of the body

The person named as Executor of the decedent's Will can also authorize the donation (755 ILCS 5/6-14).

If permission is obtained from a family member and there are others in the same or a higher priority, then an effort must be made to contact those people and make them aware of the proposed gift. For example, if the brother of the decedent agrees to the gift (4th in priority) and the decedent had an adult son (2nd in priority) then the son should be made aware of the gift. If the son objects, then no gift can be made. Similarly, the statute prohibits the gift if the decedent ever expressed his opposition to a donation.

## AFTER THE DONATION

If the family agrees to the donation, then once the operation is complete the body is delivered to the funeral home and prepared for burial or cremation as directed by the family. The operation does not disfigure the body so there can be an open casket viewing if the family so wishes.

Once the donation is made, the Organ Bank keeps in touch with the donor's family. If the family wishes, they will provide them with basic demographic information about the donation, such as the age, sex, marital status, number of children and occupation of the recipient of the gift.

If the recipient of the gift wishes to write to the donor's family to thank them for the gift, the Organ Bank will contact the donor's family and ask if they wish to receive the letter. If not, then the letter is kept on file in the event that the donor's family may want to read it at a later date.

# GIFT FOR EDUCATION OR RESEARCH

If the decedent signed a donor card indicating his wish to use his body for any purpose and he is not a candidate for an organ donation, then you can offer to release the body to any of the following institutions to be used for education or research:

> Anatomical Gift Association of Illinois
> 2240 West Fillmore Street
> Chicago, IL 60612
> (312) 733-5283
>
> Southern Illinois University
> School of Medicine
> Department of Anatomy
> Carbondale, IL 62901
> (618) 536-5511

You will need to call the institution to determine whether they will accept the body. Generally they will not accept bodies from those who have died from a contagious disease or from crushing injuries.

If they accept the donation, the family will need to pay for transportation of the body from the funeral home to the institution and also to pay for any forms that need to be filed. Transportation costs can vary significantly so it is important to comparison shop.

It usually takes 18 months to 2 years to complete the study. Once the project is complete the remains are cremated and *cremains* (cremated remains) returned to the family, or if the family wishes, the institution will arrange for the burial of the ashes.

# THE FUNERAL

Approximately one third of the population dies suddenly from an accident or undetected illness. Two thirds of the population die after being ill for a year or more with the most common scenario being that of an aged person dying after being ill for several months. In such cases, the death is expected. Family and friends are emotionally prepared for the happening. Whether expected or unexpected, the first job is the disposition of the body.

## THE PRE-ARRANGED FUNERAL

Increasingly, people are making advance arrangements for their own funeral and burial. This makes it easier on the family both financially and emotionally. All decisions have been made and there is no guessing what the decedent would have wanted.

If the decedent made provision for his burial space, then you need to locate the burial certificate. If the decedent purchased a Preneed Funeral Plan, then you need to locate the contract. You should read the contract to determine what provisions were made. Some contracts are paid on an installment basis. If the decedent signed such a contract, then you need to find out what monies were paid and whether there is a remaining balance due.

If you cannot locate the contract, but you know the name of the funeral home, then call and ask them to send you a copy of the contract. If you believe the decedent purchased a preneed plan but you do not know the name of the funeral home, then call the local funeral homes. Many local funeral homes are owned by national firms with computer capacity to identify people who have purchased a contract in any of their many locations.

Once you have possession of the contract, bring it with you to the funeral home and go over the terms of the contract with the funeral director. Inquire whether there will be any charge that is not included in the contract.

## MAKING FUNERAL ARRANGEMENTS

If the decedent died unexpectedly or without having made any prior funeral arrangements then your first job is to chose a funeral director and make arrangements for the funeral or cremation. Most people choose the nearest or most conveniently located funeral home without comparison shopping, however prices for these services can vary significantly from funeral home to funeral home. Savings can be had if you take the time to make a few phone calls.

Receiving price quotes by telephone is your right under Federal law. Federal Trade Commission ("FTC") Rule 453.2 (b)(1) requires a funeral director to give an accurate telephone quote of the prices of his goods and services. Funeral homes are listed in the telephone directory under FUNERAL DIRECTORS. If you live in a small town, there may be only one or two listings. If such is the case, then check out funeral homes in the next largest city.

Funeral Directors usually provide the following services:
➢ arrange for the transportation of the body
   to the funeral home and then to the burial site
➢ obtain burial transit permits
➢ arrange for the embalming or cremation of the body
➢ arrange funeral and memorial services
   and the viewing of the body
➢ arrange to have the obituary printed
➢ order copies of the death certificate for the family
➢ have acknowledgment and memorial cards printed.

To compare prices you will need to determine:
- ✧ what is included in the price of a basic funeral plan
- ✧ whether you can expect any additional cost.

It may be necessary to have the body embalmed if you are going to have a viewing. Embalming is not necessary if you order a direct cremation or an immediate burial. Federal Trade Commission Rule 453.5 prohibits the funeral home from charging an embalming fee unless you order the service.

If the decedent did not own a burial space, then that cost must be included when making funeral arrangements.

## PURCHASING THE CASKET

When comparison-shopping, you will find that the single most expensive item in the funeral arrangement is the casket. Most funeral directors will quote you a price for the basic funeral plan. That plan does not include the cost of the casket. Directors usually quote a range of prices for the casket, saying that you will need to come in and choose the casket at the time you contract for the funeral.

When selecting a casket you should be aware that there is often a considerable markup in the price quoted by the funeral director. You do not need to deal "sole source" in the purchase of the casket. You can purchase a casket elsewhere and have it delivered to the funeral home for use instead of the one offered by the funeral director.

In 1994, The Federal Trade Commission ruled that funeral homes had to accept caskets purchased elsewhere. (FTC Rule 453.4). The ruling includes a ban on funeral homes charging a handling fee for accepting a casket purchased elsewhere.

If you wish to shop for a casket, then the best time to do so is before you go to the funeral home to arrange for the funeral. You can find a retail casket sales outlet in the telephone book under CASKETS. You may need to look in the telephone directory for the nearest large city to find a listing.  For users of the Internet, you can use your search engine to find the retail sales casket company nearest you. By making a call to a retail casket sales dealer, you will become knowledgeable in the price range of caskets.  You can then decide what is a reasonable price for the product you seek.

Once you have determined what you should pay for the casket, it is only fair to give the funeral director the opportunity to meet that price. If you cannot reach a meeting of the minds, then you can always order the casket from the retail sales dealer and have it delivered to the funeral home.

## OTHER ON-LINE FUNERAL SERVICES
The Internet is changing the way the world does business, and the funeral industry is no exception. A growing number of mortuaries are offering live Webcasts of funerals and wakes for those who are unable to pay their respects in person.

There are Web sites that offer online memorials, obituary notices as well as online eulogies and testimonials.  There is even  a Web site that offers a posthumous e-mail service which allows people to leave final messages for friends and relatives.

# THE CREMATION

Increasingly people are opting for cremation. The reasons for choosing cremation are varied, but for the majority, it is a matter of finances. The cost of cremation is about one-sixth that of an ordinary funeral and burial. A major saving is the cost of the casket. No casket is necessary for the cremation. Illinois law prohibits a Funeral Director from requiring that you buy a casket when the body is being cremated (225 ILCS 41/15-75 (b)12). Of course if you want to have a viewing of the body and/or a funeral service with the body present, then you may need to purchase a disposable casket made of wood or cardboard, or you can rent a casket from the Funeral Director.

If you do not require any type of funeral service or public viewing of the body, then consider contracting with a facility that does cremations only. They are listed in the telephone book as **CREMATION SERVICES.**

Illinois law requires that if the decedent did not make a preneed arrangement for cremation, then someone must give written authorization for the cremation (spouse, executor, family member, or anyone else who is authorized to dispose of the body). If the decedent ever expressed an objection to cremation or if any family member objects to the procedure, then no cremation can take place (410 ILCS 18/15 (c).

| Special Situation | THE OVERWEIGHT DECEDENT OR ONE WITH A PACEMAKER |

If the decedent weighs more than 300 pounds, then you need to check to see if the Cremation service has facilities large enough to handle the body. If you cannot locate a crematory that can accommodate the body, then you need to make burial arrangements.

Illinois statute prohibits cremation of a decedent with a pacemaker (410 ILCS 18/35(c)). If the decedent has a pacemaker then you need to notify the cremation service and make arrangement to have the pacemaker removed prior to the cremation.

# DISPOSING OF THE ASHES

If you contract to have the decedent cremated but neglect to pick up the cremains, then 60 days after the cremation, the crematory may dispose of the cremains and charge you for their final disposition; so it is important that you make arrangements for the final disposition of the cremains within the 60 day period (410 ILCS 18/40 (d)).

You can have the decedent's cremains placed in a cemetery. Many cemeteries have a separate building called *columbarium*, which is a building especially designed to store urns. If not, then the cremains can be placed in a cemetery plot. Some cemeteries allow the cremains of a family member to be placed in a occupied family plot. Similarly, some cemeteries allow the cremains to be place in the space in a mausoleum that is currently occupied by a member of the decedent's family. If it is your desire to have the cremains placed in an occupied family plot or mausoleum, then you need to call the cemetery and ask them to explain their policy as it relates to the burial of urns in occupied sites.

If the cremains are to be placed in a cemetery, then you need to obtain a suitable urn for the burial. You can purchase the urn from the Funeral Director or Crematory Service Director. Urns cost much less than caskets, but they can cost several hundred dollars. You may wish to do some comparison shopping by calling a retail sales casket dealer.

The decedent may have expressed a desire that his ashes be spread out to sea. The Funeral Director or Cremation Service Director can assist you with such arrangements.

If the decedent is to be buried in another state, then the body will need to be transported to that state. Most funeral homes belong to a national network of funeral homes, and the out-of-state Funeral Director has the means to make local arrangements to ship the body. Contact the out-of-state Funeral Director and have him/her make arrangement with the airline for the transportation of the body.

If services are to be held in Illinois and in another state, then contact the local funeral home and they will make arrangements with the out-of-state funeral home for the shipment of the body.

If the body has been cremated, then you can transport the ashes yourself, either by carrying the ashes as part of your luggage or by arranging with the airline to transport the ashes as cargo. You should have a certified copy of the death certificate available in the event that you need to identify the remains of the decedent. Call the airline before departure and ask whether they have any special regulation or procedure to transport human ashes.

| Special Situation | THE MILITARY BURIAL |

Subject to availability of burial spaces, an honorably discharged veteran and/or his unmarried minor or handicapped child and/or his unremarried spouse may be buried in a national military cemetery. Some cemeteries have room only for cremains or for the casketed remains of a family member of someone who is currently buried in that cemetery, so you need to call to check for space availability.

Abraham Lincoln National Cemetery (at Ellwood)   (815) 423-9958

Alton National Cemetery   (314) 260-8720

Camp Butler National Cemetery (at Springfield)   (217) 492-4070

Danville National Cemetery   (217) 431-6550

Mound City National Cemetery   (314) 260-8720

Quincy National Cemetery   (309) 782-2094

Rock Island National Cemetery   (309) 782-2094

There is also a state Veterans cemetery:
Sunset Cemetery   (217) 222-8641
Illinois Veterans Home
Quincy, IL  62301

The Department of the Army is in charge of the Arlington National Cemetery. If you wish to have the decedent buried in the Arlington National Cemetery, then call them at (703) 695-3250.
Arlington National Cemetery, Interment Service Branch
Arlington, VA  22211

┌─────────────────┐
│ *Special*        \
│ *Situation*      />
└─────────────────┘

# THE COST OF A
# MILITARY BURIAL

Burial space in a National Cemetery is free of charge. Cemetery employees will open and close the grave and mark it with headstone or grave marker without cost to the family. The local Veteran's Administration ("VA") will provide the family with a memorial flag. The family needs to make funeral arrangements with a funeral firm and have them transport the remains to the cemetery.

If the decedent was receiving a VA pension then the VA will pay a burial and funeral expense allowance regardless of where the veteran is buried. The VA will not reimburse any burial or funeral cost for the spouse of a veteran.

For information about reimbursement of funeral and burial expenses you can call the VA at (800) 827-1000.

The Department of Veteran's Affairs has a web site with information about the following topics:

> ➤ National and Military Cemeteries
> ➤ Burial, Headstones and Markers
> ➤ State Cemetery Grants Program
> ➤ Obtaining Military Records
> ➤ Locating Veterans

VA CEMETERY WEB SITE
http://www.cem.va.gov

 **SPOUSE** ▶ ## BENEFITS FOR SPOUSE OF DECEDENT VETERAN

If the decedent was honorably discharged, then regardless of where he is buried, his spouse might be eligible for a contribution from the Veteran's Administration for his funeral and burial expenses. If the decedent had minor or disabled children, his spouse may also be eligible for a monthly benefit of Dependency and Indemnity Compensation ("DIC").

If the Veteran's surviving spouse receives nursing home care under Medicaid, then the spouse might be eligible for a monthly payment from the VA. Whether a surviving spouse is eligible for any of these benefits depends on many factors including whether the decedent was serving on active duty, whether his death was service related, and the surviving spouse's assets and income.

For information about whether the surviving spouse is eligible for any benefit related to the decedent's military service, call the VETERANS ADMINISTRATION at (800) 827-1000.

You can receive a printed statement of public policy: VA Pamphlet 051-000-00217-2 FEDERAL BENEFITS FOR VETERANS AND DEPENDENTS by sending a check in the amount of $5 to THE SUPERINTENDENT OF DOCUMENTS
P.O. Box 371954
Pittsburgh, PA 15250-7954
Information is also available on the VA web site:

 **VA WEB SITE**
http://www.va.gov

## THE PROBLEM
## FUNERAL OR BURIAL

The funeral and burial industry is well regulated by the state and federal government. Under Illinois statute (225 ILCS 41/15-75) the following acts are subject to disciplinary action:

⊠ Delivering goods of a lesser quality than that presented to the purchaser as a sample

⊠ Using a false or misleading advertisement

⊠ Paying kickbacks to generate business

⊠ Treating anyone differently because of race, color, creed, sex, religion or national origin

⊠ Soliciting human bodies after death or while death is imminent

⊠ Continued practice by a person having an infectious or contagious disease

Funeral directors are licensed professionals so it is unusual to have a problem with the funeral or burial or cremation. If, however, you had a bad experience with any aspect of the funeral then you can file a complaint with the state licensing agency:

Professional Services Section
Department of Professional Regulation
320 W. Washington Street
Springfield, IL 62786
(217) 782-0458

 **LAWYER**

If you are not satisfied with the results obtained with the state agency, then consult with an attorney who is experienced in litigation matters.

Each county has the duty to bury anyone who dies in that county and who is without sufficient funds for burial. If an indigent person dies and the police know his identity, they will try to locate the family. If the identity of the decedent unknown, or if his family is unable or unwilling to arrange for his burial, then whoever is in charge of the body (jailors, sheriffs, coroners, funeral directors, etc.) is required to surrender the body to any medical school that requests a donation for the purpose of the advancement of science. Before doing so, the person in charge of the body must give notice of the donation to the family or guardian of the decedent. If the family wants to bury the body, then they can do so and the donation will not be made. Similarly, if the decedent left a Will stating his wishes as to the disposition of his remains, then the donation cannot be made unless it was the decedent's wish to do so (410 ILCS 510/1).

## THE INDIGENT VETERAN AND HIS FAMILY

If the decedent was an honorably discharged veteran, then the family can arrange to have Veteran's burial. If the family wishes they can arrange to have the veteran buried in a cemetery in the county in which he died. The county will pay up to $600 to bury the indigent veteran. If the parent, spouse, widow, widower, minor child of a honorably discharged veteran dies without sufficient funds for burial, then the county will bury that member of the veteran's family, provided the member of the family was not receiving public assistance funds at the time of his/her death (55 ILCS 5/5-27001, 27002).

 LAWYER

# THE VIOLENT DEATH OR ACCIDENTAL DEATH

If the decedent died a violent death or under circumstances in which foul play is suspected, the Coroner or Medical Examiner will take possession of the body. The body will not be released to the funeral director until the examination of the body is complete. In the interim, the family can proceed with arrangements for the funeral. The funeral director will contact the Coroner or Medical Examiner to determine when the body can be picked up.

If the decedent died because of an accident then it is important to contact a Personal Injury attorney to determine whether the family can be compensated for their loss. If the accident was related to the decedent's job, you may wish to consult with a Worker's Compensation attorney as well.

If the decedent died because of a criminal act, then consider contacting an attorney experienced in Criminal Law to learn of your rights as a family member. If the perpetrator of the crime has significant funds, you may want to sue for wrongful death.

# COMPENSATION FOR THE VICTIM

If the decedent died because of a criminal act and you are a family member, then you may be eligible to receive compensation under the ILLINOIS CRIME VICTIMS COMPENSATION ACT (740 ILCS 45). The state provides compensation for reasonable funeral expenses (up to $3,000) and/or medical expenses. Total compensation may not exceed $25,000. To be eligible the following must be true:

➤ The decedent was an Illinois resident.

➤ The decedent was an innocent victim (i.e., did not do anything wrong).

➤ The crime was reported to authorities within 72 hours of its commission or discovery of the body.

➤ There was full cooperation with law enforcement officers by the victim and/or his family.

➤ Application for compensation was filed within one year from the injury or death.

➤ There are no other resources, such as health or life insurance, available to cover medical or burial costs.

To receive an application for compensation, you can call (800) 228-3368. For the hearing impaired call TTY: (312) 814-3374 or write to:

CRIME VICTIMS COMPENSATION PROGRAM
100 West Randolph Street
Chicago, IL 60601

 **LAWYER** THE MISSING PERSON

Few things are more difficult to deal with than a missing person. The emotional turmoil created by the "not knowing" is often more difficult than the finality of death. The legal problems created by the disappearance are also more difficult than if the person simply died. It may take a two-part legal process — a procedure called *Administration To Collect*, to handle the missing person's affairs while he is missing and then a final probate procedure if he is later found dead or declared to be dead.

If the missing person had a Will, then the judge in the Probate section of the Circuit Court will usually appoint the person named as Executor, to be the Administrator to Collect. If the missing person did not have a Will, then the court will appoint the person with priority to settle the person's estate. See page 27 for the list of persons with priority. The court appointed Administrator will collect all of the missing persons assets and pay bills and/or support the missing persons family, all under court supervision (755 ILCS 5/10-1 and 5/10-4).

If it is necessary to have an Administrator appointed to manage his affairs, then you need to employ an attorney to present evidence to the court that the person is missing and that there is a pressing need to manage the missing person's affairs. If there is no need to manage the person's affairs, then probate can begin after 7 years. Courts in Illinois have ruled that a person is presumed dead if 7 years have passed and he cannot be located after a diligent search has been made (In Re Estate of King 304 Ill. App.3d 479 (1999) 710 N.E.2d 1249)

# THE DEATH CERTIFICATE

The Funeral Director or Cremation Service Director will order as many death certificates as you request. Most establishments require an original certified copy and not a photocopy so you need to order sufficient certified copies.

The following is a list of institutions that may want a certified copy:

* Each insurance company that insured the decedent or his property (health insurance company, life insurance company, car insurance company, home insurance company)

* Each financial institution in which the decedent had money invested (brokerage houses, banks)

* The decedent's pension fund

* Each credit card company used by the decedent

* The IRS

* The Social Security Administration

* The County Recorder in each county where the decedent owned real property.

Some airlines and car rental companies offer a discount for short notice, emergency trips. If you have family flying in for the funeral, you may wish to order a few extra copies of the death certificate so that they can obtain an airline or car rental discount.

# ORDERING COPIES OF THE DEATH CERTIFICATE

If you wish to order certified copies of the death certificate at a later date, you can call the funeral director and ask him to do so or you can get copies from the courthouse in the county of the decedent's residence.

You can also get certified copies of the death certificate by writing to:

> Division of Vital Records
> 605 W. Jefferson Street
> Springfield, IL  62702-5097
> Telephone: (217) 782-6553

The present charge is $17 for the first certified copy and $2 for each certified copy ordered at the same time. They accept personal checks or money orders made payable to the Illinois Department of Public Health.

They will provide copies to family members or the person named as Executor of the Will or whoever is appointed by the Probate court to settle the decedent's estate. You need to first call and ask and asking what information they require. The current turn-around time is 30 days but if you send your request by overnight express mail, they will forward it to you within 2 business days.

You can also obtain a certified copy of the death certificate from the county courthouse. Call the clerk in the county of the decedent's residence for information as to the cost and time it takes to get copies of the death certificate.

# RECORDING THE DEATH CERTIFICATE

In Illinois, the Department of Public Health issues the death certificate. The Department does not publish the death certificate so it is not part of the public record. If the decedent owned real property, then the death certificate may need to be recorded in the county where the decedent owned property so that anyone who is examining title to the property will know that the owner of the property died.

We will be discussing how to transfer real property in Chapter 6. You will find that, in many cases, you will need the assistance of an attorney to transfer the decedent's real property to the proper beneficiary. The attorney will arrange for the recording of whatever documentation is necessary in order to transfer title.

---

 LAWYER

## DECEDENT WITH OUT OF STATE PROPERTY

If the decedent owned property in another state, then a death certificate may need to be recorded in the county where that property is located. Not all states require that the death certificate be recorded. You may want to call the Clerk to determine whether a death certificate needs to be recorded. In some states the county Registrar or the Clerk of the Circuit Court is in charge of recording deeds (and death certificates).

If you find that a death certificate needs to be recorded, it is prudent to contact an attorney in the state where the property is located for advise about what other document may need to be recorded in order to transfer the decedent's real property in that state.

---

# About Probate

Once a person dies, all of the property he owns as of the date of his death is referred to as the decedent's *estate*. If the decedent owned property that was in his name only (not jointly or in trust for someone) then some sort of court procedure is necessary to determine who is entitled to possession of the property. The name of the court procedure is *probate.*

There are different ways to conduct a probate procedure depending on the value of the probate estate and whether the decedent owned real property at the time of his death. The method of conducting a probate procedure is call the *estate administration*. Chapter 6 explains how to determine whether a probate procedure is necessary and if so, then what kind of estate administration is necessary.

The root of the word probate is "to prove." It refers to the first job of the probate court, that is, to examine proof of whether the decedent left a valid Will or whether the decedent died without a Will. The second job of the probate court is to appoint someone to wrap up the affairs of the decedent — to pay any outstanding bills and then to distribute what property is left to the beneficiaries. If the decedent left a Will, then the person he named as *Executor* will be appointed to do the job. The court will issue *Letters Testamentary* giving the Executor authority to act. If he died intestate, then the court will appoint an *Administrator* to settle the estate and give him *Letters of Administration*. For simplicity, we will refer to the person appointed by the court to settle the decedent's estate as the *Decedent's Representative* and *Letters* to describe the court document that give the Representative authority to act.

Whether a probate procedure is necessary or not, the first order of business is to give notice of the death, and that is explained in the next chapter.

# Giving Notice Of The Death  2

Those closest to the decedent usually notify family members and close friends by telephone. The funeral director will arrange to publish an obituary in as many different newspapers as the family requests, but there is still the job of notifying the government and people who were doing business with the decedent. That task belongs to the person named as Executor in the decedent's Will. If the decedent died without a Will and a probate procedure is necessary, then the court will appoint the Decedent's Representative using the order of priority as stated in Illinois statute 755 ILCS 5/9-3:

1. the spouse
2. anyone who inherits the decedent's property,
   with preference give to the decedent's children
3. the decedent's children   4. the grandchildren
5. the parents                  6. the brothers and sisters
7. the nearest kindred (blood relation)

Anyone with priority can do the job themselves or they can appoint someone to be the Representative in their place.

If no probate procedure is necessary, the job of notifying people of the death and settling the decedent's affairs falls to his spouse; and in the absence of a spouse, to the decedent's next of kin. By **next of kin**, we mean those people who inherit the decedent's property according to the Illinois Rules of Descent and Distribution. That law is explained in Chapter 5. The person who has the job of settling the decedent's estate should begin to give notice as soon as is practicable after the death. Two government agencies that need to be notified are the Social Security Administration and the IRS.

# NOTIFYING SOCIAL SECURITY

Many Funeral Directors will, as part of their service package, notify the Social Security Administration of the death. You may wish to check to see that this has been done. You can do so by calling (800) 772-1213. If you are hearing impaired call (800) 325-0778 TTY. You will need to give the Social Security Administration the full legal name of the decedent as well as his social security number and date of birth.

---

*Special Situation* ⟩ **FOR DECEDENT RECEIVING SOCIAL SECURITY CHECKS**

If the decedent was receiving checks from Social Security, then you need to determine whether his last check needs to be returned to the Social Security Administration. Each Social Security check is a payment for the prior month, provided that person lives for the entire prior month. If someone dies on the last day of the month, then you should not cash the check for that month. For example, if someone dies on July 31st, then you need to return the check that the agency mails out in August. If however, the decedent died on August 1st then the check sent in August need not be returned because that check is payment for the month of July.

If the Social Security check is electronically deposited into a bank account then notify the bank that the account holder died and notify the Social Security Administration as well. If the check needs to be returned, then the Social Security Administration will withdraw it electronically from the bank account. You will need to keep the account open until the funds are withdrawn.

---

 **SPOUSE**

# SPOUSE and CHILD'S
# SOCIAL SECURITY BENEFITS

If the decedent had sufficient work credits, the Social Security Administration will give the decedent's widow(er) or if unmarried, then the decedent's minor children, a one-time death benefit in the amount of $255.

## SURVIVORS BENEFITS:

The spouse (or ex-spouse) of the decedent may be eligible for Survivors Benefits. Benefits vary depending on the amount of work credits earned by the decedent; whether the decedent had minor or disabled children; the spouse's age; how long they were married; etc.

The minor child of the decedent may be eligible for dependent child's benefits regardless of whether the decedent father ever married the child's mother. Paternity can be established by any one of several methods including the father acknowledging his child in writing or verbally to members of his family.

## SOCIAL SECURITY BENEFITS

A spouse or ex-spouse can collect social security benefits based on the decedent's work record. This value may be greater than the spouse now receives. It is important to make an appointment with your local Social Security office and determine whether you as the spouse (or ex-spouse), or parent of the decedent's minor child, are eligible for Social Security or Survivor benefits. The SOCIAL SECURITY ADMINISTRATION has a Web site from which you can down load publications that explain social security and survivor benefits.

 **SOCIAL SECURITY WEB SITE**
http://www.ssa.gov

> **Special Situation**

# DECEDENT WITH GOVERNMENT PENSION

If the decedent was a federal retiree and received a government pension then any check received after the date of death needs to be returned to the U.S. Treasury. If the check is direct deposited to a bank account, then call the financial institution and ask them to return the check. If the check is sent by mail then you need to return it to: Director, Regional Finance Center

U. S. Treasury Department
P.O. Box 7367
Chicago, IL 60680

Include a letter explaining the reason for the return of the check and stating the decedent's date of death.

## $$$ APPLY FOR BENEFITS $$$

Even though you notify the government of the death, they will not automatically give you benefits to which you may be entitled. You need to apply for those benefits by notifying the Office of Personnel Management ("OPM") of the death and requesting that they send you an application for survivor benefits. You can call them at (888) 767-6738 or you can write to:

THE OFFICE OF PERSONNEL MANAGEMENT SERVICE
AND RECORDS CENTER
BOYERS, PA 16017

You will find brochures and information about Survivor's Benefits at the Office's Web site:

**OPM WEB SITE**
http://www.opm.gov
You can get assistance via E-mail at
retire@opm.gov

In most cases, pension and annuity checks are payment for the prior month. If the decedent received his pension or annuity check before his death, then no monies need be returned. Pension checks and/or annuity checks received after the date of death may need to be returned to the company. You need to notify the company of the death to determine the status of the last check sent to the decedent.

Before notifying the company, locate the policy or pension statement that is the basis of the income. That document should tell whether there is a beneficiary of the pension or annuity funds now that the pensioner or annuitant is dead. If you cannot locate the document, use the return address on the check envelope and ask the company to send you a copy of the plan. Also request that they forward to you any claim form that may be required in order for the survivor or beneficiary to receive benefits under that pension plan or policy.

If the pension/annuity check is direct deposited to the decedent's account, then ask the bank to assist you in locating the company and notifying the company of the death.

> **Special Situation** | # DECEDENT WITH AN IRA OR QRP ACCOUNT

Anyone who is a beneficiary of an Individual Retirement Account ("IRA") or Qualified Retirement Plan ("QRP") needs to keep in mind that no income taxes have been paid on monies placed in an IRA or QRP account. Once monies are withdrawn, significant taxes may be due. You need to learn what options are available to you as a beneficiary of the plan and the tax consequences of each option. You need to ask an accountant how much will be due in taxes for each option. Once you know all the facts, you will be able to make the best choice for your set of circumstances.

 **SPOUSE** If the spouse is the beneficiary of the decedent's IRA account, then there are special options available. The spouse has the right to withdraw the money from the account or roll it over into the spouse's own retirement account. Although the employer can explain options that are available, the spouse still needs to understand the tax consequence of choosing any given option. It is important to consult with an accountant to determine the best way to go.

If the decedent had a QRP, the plan may permit the spouse to roll the balance of the account into a new IRA. The spouse needs to contact the decedent's employer for an explanation of the plan and all the options that are available at this time.

# NOTIFYING IRS

## THE FINAL INCOME TAX RETURN

The Decedent's Representative, or next of kin, needs to file the decedent's final state and federal income tax returns. This can be done as part of the income tax return for the year of his death. If you have a joint bank account with the decedent, do not close that account until you determine whether the decedent is entitled to an income tax refund. See Chapter 6 for an explanation of how to obtain a refund from the IRS and from the state.

## THE GOOD NEWS

Monies inherited from the decedent are not counted as income to you, so you do not pay federal income tax on those monies. If the monies you inherit later earn interest or income for you, then of course you will report that income as you do any other type of income.

Real and personal property inherited by a beneficiary is inherited at a "stepped up" basis. This means that if the decedent purchased some item that is now worth more than when he purchased it, then the beneficiary inherits the property at its fair market value as of the decedent's date of death. For example, suppose the decedent bought stock for $20,000 and it is now worth $50,000, then the beneficiary inherits the stock at the $50,000 value If the beneficiary sells the stock for $50,000, he pays no tax. If the beneficiary holds onto the stock and later sells it for $60,000, the beneficiary will pay federal capital gains tax only on the $10,000 increase in value since the decedent's death.

## WHEN TO EVALUATE THE PROPERTY

The IRS gives you a choice of taking the value of the decedent's estate as of his date of death or 6 months later. For example, suppose the decedent's estate consists of stock worth $100,000 and you decide to hold onto them. If they increase in value so that 6 months later they are worth 110,000, you can (by filing the proper IRS tax return) elect to evaluate the decedent's estate at the six-month value in place of the date-of-death value. If you sell the stock at that time then you will not pay capital gains on the stock.

 If you hold onto the stock there is a risk that it will decrease in value during that six month period.

If the stock goes down to $80,000, and you then sell, your only consolation will be that you can reflect the loss on your income tax statement.

Also, you need to consider the cost of employing an accountant (or a tax attorney) to file the necessary forms for the 6-month election. If you hold onto the stock and the increase in value is only a few thousand dollars, it may not pay to take the election. The cost in time and expense to make the election could be more than the tax payment itself.

 **SPOUSE** | # WIDOW'S HOMESTEAD TAX BENEFITS

Illinois statute gives a disabled veteran a homestead tax exemption for property up to $50,000 in value. The spouse of a decedent disabled veteran is entitled to the same tax exemption for as long as the spouse remains unmarried. The exemption is lost once the widow(er) marries (35 ILCS 200/15-165).

If the decedent was 65 years of age or older, and owned his home, then he qualified for a Senior Citizens Homestead exemption. If the spouse inherits the decedent's share of the homestead, then the spouse is eligible for the same exemption, even if the spouse does not meet the age criteria (35 ILCS 200/15-172(c)).

For information about how to apply for the homestead tax exemption you need to call the Chief County Assessment Officer or Assessor in the county where the homestead is located.

## CAPITAL GAINS EXCLUSION

In the tough "ole days" the IRS used to allow a once-in-a-lifetime, over age 55, up to $125,000 capital gains tax exclusion on the sale of the homestead. If a married couple sold their home and took the exclusion it was "used up" and no longer available to the other partner. In these, the good times, the IRS allows you to sell your homestead and up to $250,000 ($500,000 for a married couple of the home-sale profit is tax free (IRC Section 121 B 3). There is no limit on the number of times you can use the exemption, provided you own and live in the homestead at least 2 years prior to the sale. If the decedent and his spouse used their "once in a lifetime" homestead tax exemption, with this new law, the surviving spouse can sell the homestead and once again take advantage of a tax break.

An *estate tax* is a tax imposed by the federal and state government for the transfer of property at death. The *taxable estate* of the decedent is the total value of all of his property, as of his date of death. This includes real property (homestead, vacant lots, etc.) and personal property (cars, life insurance policies, business interests, securities, IRA accounts, etc.). It includes property held in the decedent's name alone, as well as property that he held jointly or in trust for another.

The Federal government gives each person an Estate and Gift Tax Exclusion amount. No gift tax need be paid unless the decedent's taxable estate, plus gifts that he gave during his lifetime exceeding $10,000/per person per year, exceed the Exclusion amount. The Exclusion amount is scheduled to increase each year until the year 2006:

| YEAR | EXCLUSION AMOUNT |
|------|------------------|
| 2000 — 2001 | $675,000 |
| 2002 — 2003 | $700,000 |
| 2004 | $850,000 |
| 2005 | $950,000 |
| 2006 | $1,000,000 |

No Illinois Estate tax return or Federal Estate tax return need be filed unless the decedent's taxable estate and lifetime gifts exceed the scheduled amount as of his date of death (35 ILCS 405/3b). If the decedent's taxable estate exceeds the Unified Credit, then you need to employ an accountant to prepare both the Federal estate tax return (form 706) and Illinois Estate tax return (form 700). There is an unlimited marital tax deduction, so if the decedent was married, no estate tax need be paid; however if the decedent's estate exceeds the stated value, the estate tax return must be filed.

# DECEDENT WITH A TRUST

If the decedent was the Grantor (or Settlor) of a trust, then he was probably managing the trust, as Trustee, during his lifetime. The trust document should name someone as *Successor Trustee* to manage the trust now that the Grantor is deceased. The trust document may instruct the Successor Trustee to make certain gifts once the Grantor dies, or perhaps hold money in trust for a beneficiary of the trust.

## IF YOU ARE SUCCESSOR TRUSTEE

If you are the Successor Trustee then in addition to following the terms of the trust, you are required to obey all of the rules and provisions of the Illinois Trust and Trustees Act (760 ILCS 5). For example, you are required to give a full annual accounting (including an inventory of the trust) to all of the beneficiaries who are entitled to receive income from the trust (760 ILCS 5/11). You should consult with an attorney experienced in Estate Planning to explain how to properly administer the trust and to ensure that you do so without any liability to yourself.

## IF YOU ARE A BENEFICIARY

If you are a beneficiary of the trust, then you need to obtain a copy of the trust and see how the trust is to be administered now that the Grantor or Settlor is deceased. Most trust documents are written in "legalese," so you may want to employ your own attorney to review the trust, and explain what rights you have under that trust.

# NOTIFYING THE BUSINESS COMMUNITY

People and companies who were doing business with the decedent need to be notified of his death. This includes utility companies, credit card companies, banks, brokerage firms and any company that insured the decedent.

## NOTIFY CREDIT CARD COMPANIES

You need to notify the decedent's credit card companies of the death. If you can find the contract with the credit card company check to see whether the decedent had credit card insurance. If the decedent had credit card insurance, then the balance of the account is now paid in full. If you cannot find the contract contact the company and get a copy of the contract along with a statement of the balance due as of the date of death.

### DESTROY DECEDENT'S CREDIT CARDS

You should destroy all of the decedent's credit cards. If you hold a credit card jointly with the decedent, then it is important to waste no time in closing that account and opening another in your name only. That's a lesson Barbara learned from hard experience. She and Hank never married but they did live together for several years before he died from liver disease. Hank came from a well to do family so he had enough money to support himself and Barbara during his long illness.

Hank put Barbara on all of his credit card accounts so that she could purchase things when he became too ill to go shopping with her. After the funeral, Barbara had a gathering of friends and family at their apartment. Barbara was so preoccupied with her loss that she never noticed that the credit cards were missing until the bills started coming in.

Barbara did not know who ran up the bills on Hank's credit cards during the month following his death. It was obvious that his signature had been forged — but who forged it? One credit card company suspected that it might have been Barbara herself.

Because the credit cards were held jointly, Barbara became liable to either pay the debt or prove that she did not make the purchases. She was able to clear her credit record but it took several months and she had to employ an attorney to do so.

# NOTIFY INSURANCE COMPANIES

Examine the decedent's financial records to determine the name and telephone number of all of the companies that insured the decedent or his property. This includes real property insurance, motor vehicle insurance, health insurance and life insurance.

## MOTOR VEHICLE INSURANCE

If the decedent owned any type of motor vehicle (car, truck, boat, airplane) locate the insurance policy on that vehicle and notify the insurance company of the death. Determine how long insurance coverage continues after the death. Ask the insurance agent to explain what things are covered under the policy. Is the motor vehicle covered for all types of casualty (theft, accident, vandalism, etc.) or is coverage limited in some way?

If you can continue coverage then determine when the next insurance payment is due. Hopefully, the car will be sold or transferred to a beneficiary before that date, but if not, then you need to arrange to continue with insurance coverage.

If the decedent died as a result of an accident, then check for all possible sources of accident insurance coverage. If he died at home then check the homeowner's policy. Examine all credit card contracts. Some credit card companies provide free accident insurance as part of their contract with their card holders.

If the decedent died in an automobile accident, then check to see whether he was covered by any type of travel insurance, such as rental car insurance. If he belonged to an automobile club, such as AAA, then check whether he had insurance as part of his club membership.

# LIFE INSURANCE

If the decedent had life insurance, then you need to locate the policy and notify the company of his death. Call each life insurance company and ask what they require in order to forward the insurance proceeds to the beneficiary. Most companies will ask you to send them the original policy and a certified copy of the death certificate.

Send the original policy by certified mail or any of the overnight services that require a signed receipt for the package. Make a copy of the original policy for your records before mailing the original policy to the company.

## IF YOU CANNOT LOCATE THE POLICY

If you know that the decedent was insured but you cannot locate the insurance policy, the AMERICAN COUNCIL OF LIFE INSURANCE ("ACLI") may be able to help you. Write to the ACLI giving them the name, address, date of birth, and social security number of the decedent. Their address is:

POLICY SEARCH ACLI
1000 Pennsylvania Avenue, NW
Washington, DC 20004

The ACLI will assist you by asking the 100 largest insurance companies in the nation to search their records for the missing policy. If it is found, you will receive a copy of the policy free of charge.

# IF YOU CANNOT LOCATE THE COMPANY

If you cannot locate the insurance company it may be doing business under another name or it may no longer be doing business in the state of Illinois. Insurance companies are highly regulated. Each state has a branch of government that regulates insurance companies. If you are having difficulty locating the insurance company call the Department of Insurance in the state where the policy was purchased and ask for assistance in locating the company. The number for the Illinois Department of Insurance is (217) 782-4515.

 EAGLE PUBLISHING COMPANY OF BOCA's Web site gives the telephone number of the Department of Insurance for each state: http://www.eaglepublishing.com

# WORK RELATED INSURANCE

If the decedent was employed then his employer may provide survivor benefits from a company or group life insurance plan and/or a retirement plan. If the decedent belonged to a union, then check with the union to determine whether members of the union receive any death benefits.

The decedent may have belonged to a professional, fraternal or social organization such as the local Chamber of Commerce, a Veteran's organization, the Kiwanis, AARP, the Rotary Club, etc. If he belonged to such an organization check to see whether the organization provided any type of insurance coverage.

If the decedent owned his own company he may have purchased "key man" insurance. Key man insurance is a life insurance policy designed to protect the company should a valuable employee die. Benefits are paid to the company to compensate the company for the loss of someone who is essential to the continuation of the business. Ultimately the policy benefits those who inherit the business.

If the decedent owned shares in the company or was a partner in the company, there may be a shareholder's agreement or partnership agreement that requires the company to use the insurance proceeds to purchase the shares or buy out the partnership interest owned by the decedent. If there is a probate procedure, then the Decedent's Representative's attorney will need to review the agreement. If the decedent died without a Will, then the next of kin needs to investigate the matter to determine what rights (if any) the family has in the business or to the proceeds of the key man insurance policy.

If the decedent was the sole owner and officer of a corporation then the Illinois Secretary of State, Business Services, needs to be notified of the change. There may need to be a probate procedure to determine the new owner of the company so it may take some period of time before new officers and directors are identified.

If the decedent was the Registered Agent of a corporation, then a new agent needs to be appointed and the Secretary of State advised of the change (805 ILCS 5/5.10).

Forms to change officers and statutory agents can be obtained by calling (800) 252-8980. If you are calling from another state then call (217) 782-7800.

STATUS REPORT

If you were not actively involved in running the business, then you can request an abstract of the corporate record from Business Services (805 ILCS 5/1.30). The report will show whether filing fees are current and will identify the officers and directors of the company. You will need to request the information in writing, so you may wish to call Business Services at the above number to determine what information and fee they require.

## HOMEOWNER INSURANCE

If the decedent owned his own home, then check whether there is sufficient insurance coverage on the property. The decedent may have neglected to increase his insurance as the property appreciated in value. If you think the property may be vacant for some period of time, then consider having vandalism coverage included in the policy.

Once the property is sold, or transferred to the proper beneficiary, you can have the policy discontinued or transferred to the new owner. The decedent's estate should receive a rebate for the unused portion of the premium.

## NOTIFYING THE HOMEOWNER'S ASSOCIATION

If the decedent owned a condominium or a residence regulated by a homeowner's association, then the association needs to be notified of the death. Once the property is transferred to the proper beneficiary, he/she will need to contact the association and arrange to have notices of dues or assessments forwarded to the new owner.

## MORTGAGE INSURANCE

If the decedent had a mortgage on any parcel of real estate that he owned, he might have arranged with his lender for an insurance policy that pays off the mortgage balance in the event of his death. Look at the closing statement to see if there was a charge for mortgage insurance. Also, check with the lender to determine if such a policy was purchased.

If the decedent was the sole owner of the property, then the beneficiary of that property needs to make arrangements to continue payment of the mortgage until title to the property is transferred to that beneficiary.

# HEALTH INSURANCE

If the decedent had health insurance coverage, then the insurance carrier probably knows of the death, but it is a good idea to contact them to determine what coverage the decedent had under that insurance plan. If you cannot find the original policy, have the insurance company send you a copy of the policy so that you can determine whether medical treatment  rendered to the decedent before his death was covered by that policy.

## DECEDENT ON MEDICARE

If the decedent was covered by Medicare, you do not need to notify anyone, but you do need to know what things were covered by Medicare so that you can determine what medical bills are (or are not)  covered by Medicare.  The publication MEDICARE AND YOU explains what things are covered.  You can get it the publication by writing to:

U.S. GOVERNMENT PRINTING OFFICE
U.S. Dept. of Health and Human Services
Health Care Financing Administration
7500 Security Boulevard
Baltimore, MD  21244-1850

You can also find the publication on the Internet:

MEDICARE WEB SITE
http:/www.medicare.gov

If you have questions  about Medicare  coverage, there is a toll-free Medicare Hotline (800)633-4227. English and Spanish speaking operators are available Monday through Friday from  8 a.m. to 4:30 p.m.  For the hearing  impaired call TTY/TDD (877) 486-2048.

## THE SPOUSE'S HEALTH INSURANCE

If the spouse of the decedent is insured under Medicare, then the death does not affect the surviving spouse's coverage. If the surviving spouse has her own health insurance and the decedent was covered under that plan, the spouse needs to notify her employer of the death because this may affect the cost of the plan to the employer and/or the spouse.

If the spouse was covered under the decedent's policy then he/she needs to arrange for new coverage. Both the federal and state government require that the employer make the company health plan available to the surviving spouse and dependent children.

### CONTINUED COVERAGE UNDER COBRA

If the decedent was employed by a company with at least twenty employees then the company falls under federal as well as state regulation (The Consolidated Omnibus Budget Reconciliation Act ("COBRA"). The rules under COBRA differ from the state regulation. Regardless of whether the company is regulated by the state or federal government, it is important that the spouse notify the company as soon as possible after the death to ensure continued health care coverage.

You can find additional information about COBRA in the pamphlet PENSION AND HEALTH CARE COVERAGE as well as other information about the U.S. Department of Labor publications at their Web site:

DEPARTMENT OF LABOR WEB SITE
http://www.dol.gov/dol/pwba

# CONTINUED COVERAGE UNDER ILLINOIS LAW

If the decedent's employer has less than 20 employees, then the spouse can continue coverage under the Illinois Health Insurance Portability and Accountability Act. Illinois statute requires that within 30 days of the death, the spouse must give the company written notice that the employee died.

The employer must, within 15 days of receiving the notice, report the death to the insurance company and send a copy of the report to the spouse. The insurance company then has 30 days to offer health insurance coverage to the spouse. They must notify the spouse of the cost of the policy and must include a form to accept the insurance policy. If the spouse does not accept within 30 days, then the right to continue insurance benefits is terminated (215 ILCS 5/367.2).

# ✍ CHANGE BENEFICIARY ✍

If the decedent was someone that you named as your beneficiary in an insurance policy, security, Will or pension plan, then you may need to name another beneficiary in his place:

## INSURANCE POLICY ✍

If you named the decedent as the primary beneficiary of your life insurance policy, then check to see whether you named an alternate beneficiary in the event that the decedent did not survive you. If not, then you need to contact the insurance company to name a new beneficiary at this time.

## WILL OR TRUST ✍

Most Wills provide for an alternate beneficiary in the event that the person named as beneficiary dies first. If you named the decedent as your beneficiary, then check to see whether you named an alternate beneficiary. If not, you will need to have your attorney prepare a codicil (addendum) to your Will.

Similarly, if you are the Grantor or Settlor of a trust and the decedent was one of the beneficiaries of your trust, then check the trust document to see if you named an alternate beneficiary. If not, contact your attorney to prepare an amendment to the trust, naming a new beneficiary.

## BANK/SECURITIES ACCOUNT ✍

If the decedent was a beneficiary of your bank or securities account, or if the decedent was a joint owner of your bank account or securities account, then it is important to contact the financial institution and inform them of the death. You may wish to arrange for a new beneficiary or joint owner at this time.

## PENSION PLANS ✍

If the decedent was a beneficiary under your pension plan, then you need to notify them of his death and name a new beneficiary. Many pension plans require that you notify them within a set period of time (usually 30 days) so it is important to notify them as soon as you are able.

If the decedent was a beneficiary of your Individual Retirement Account ("IRA") or of your Qualified Retirement Plan ("QRP") and you did not provide for an alternate beneficiary, then you need to name someone at this time.

There are many government regulations relating to IRA and QRP accounts. For example, you must begin to withdraw money from the account on April 1st of the year after you reach the age of 70 1/2. How much you must withdraw depends on whether you choose to base the amount withdrawn on your own life expectancy or on the joint life expectancy of you and your oldest beneficiary.

If you have not reached the age of 70 1/2, then before naming a new beneficiary, you may wish to consult with your accountant, attorney or financial planner to decide which is the best option for you.

# NOTIFYING CREDITORS

If the decedent owed money, and a probate procedure is necessary, then it will be the job of the person who is appointed as Decedent's Representative to give written notice of the death to all of the decedent's creditors. The attorney who handles the probate will explain to the Decedent's Representative how notice is to be given.

If no probate procedure is necessary, then the next of kin can notify the creditors of the death, but before doing so, first read Chapter 4: WHAT BILLS NEED TO BE PAID? Chapter 4 explains what bills need to be paid and who is responsible to pay them, but before any bill can be paid, you need to know what the decedent owned as of his date of death. The next chapter explains how to identify, and then locate all of the property owned by the decedent.

# Locating the Assets 3

It is important to locate the financial records of the decedent and then carefully examine those records. Even the partner of a long-term marriage should conduct a thorough search because the surviving spouse may be unaware of all that was owned (or owed) by the decedent.

It is not unusual for a surviving spouse to be surprised when learning of the decedent's business transactions — especially in those cases where the decedent had control of family finances. One such example is that of Sam and Helen. They married just as soon as Sam was discharged from the army after World War II. During their marriage, Sam handled all of the finances, giving Helen just enough money to run the household.

Every now and again Helen would think of getting a job. She longed to have her own source of income and some economic independence. Each time she brought up the subject Sam would loudly object. He had no patience for this new "woman's lib" thing. Sam said he got married to have a real wife — one who would cook his meals and keep house for him.

Helen was not the arguing type. She rationalized, saying that Sam had a delicate stomach and dust allergies. He needed her to prepare his special meals and keep an immaculate house for him. Besides, Sam had a good job with a major cruise line and he needed her to accompany him on his frequent business trips.

Once Sam retired, he was even more cautious in his spending habits. Helen seldom complained. She assumed the reason for his "thrift" was that they had little money and had to live on his pension.

They were married 52 years when Sam died at the age of 83. Helen was 81 at the time of his death. She was one very happy, very angry and very aged widow when she discovered that Sam left her with assets worth well over a million dollars!

## LOCATING FINANCIAL RECORDS

To locate the decedent's assets you need to find evidence of what he owned and where those assets are located. His financial records should lead you to the location of all of his assets so your first job is to locate those records. The best place to start the search is in the decedent's home. Many people keep their financial records in a single place but it is important to check the entire house to be sure you did not miss something.

### CHECK THE COMPUTER
Don't overlook that computer sitting silently in the corner. It may hold the decedent's check register and all of the decedent's financial records. The computer may be programmed to protect information. If you cannot access the decedent's records, you may need to employ a computer technician or computer consultant who will be able to print out all of the information on the hard drive of the computer. You can find such a technician or consultant by looking in the telephone book under
COMPUTER SUPPORT SERVICES or
COMPUTER SYSTEM DESIGNS & CONSULTANTS.

# COLLECT AND IDENTIFY KEYS

The decedent may have kept his records in a safe deposit box, so you may find that your first job is to locate the keys to the box. As you go through the personal effects of the decedent, collect and identify all the keys that you find. If you come across an unidentified key, it could be a key to a post office box (private or federal) or a safe deposit box located in a bank or in a private vault company. You will need to determine whether that key opens a box that contains property belonging to the decedent or whether the key is to a box no longer in use. Some ways to investigate are as follows:

☑ CHECK BUSINESS RECORDS

If the decedent kept receipts, look through those items to see if he paid for the rental of a post office or safe deposit box. Also, check his check register to see if he wrote out a check to the Postmaster or to any safe deposit or vault company. Look at his bank statements to see if there is any bank charge for a safe deposit box. Some banks bill separately for safe deposit boxes so check with all of the banks in which the decedent had an account to determine if he had a box with that bank.

☑ CHECK THE KEY TYPE

If you cannot identify the key take the key to all of the local locksmiths and ask whether anyone can identify the type of facility that uses such keys. If that doesn't work, then go to each bank, post office and private safe deposit boxes located in places where the decedent shopped, worked or frequented and ask whether they use the type of key that you found.

☑ CHECK THE MAIL

Check the mail over the next several months to see if the decedent receives a statement requesting payment for the next year's rental of a post office or safe deposit box.

You may find evidence of a brokerage account, bank account, or safe deposit box by examining correspondence addressed to the decedent. If the decedent was living alone, then have the mail forwarded to the person he named as Decedent's Representative or executor of his Will. If the decedent did not leave a Will then the mail should be forwarded to his next of kin. Call the Postmaster and ask him/her to send you the necessary forms to make the change. Request that the mail be forwarded for the longest period allowed by law (currently one year).

The decedent may have been renting a post office box at his local post office branch or perhaps at the branch closest to where he did his banking. Ask the Postmaster to help you determine whether the decedent was renting a post office box. If so, then you need to locate the key to the box so that you can collect the decedent's mail.

---

*Special Situation* ▷ **LOST POST OFFICE BOX KEY**

If the decedent had a post office box and you cannot locate the key, then contact the local postmaster and ask him/her what documentation is needed for you to gain possession of the mail in that box. As before, you will ask the Postmaster to have all future mail addressed to that box, forwarded to the Decedent's Representative, or if there is no Will, then to the decedent's next of kin.

---

# WHAT TO DO WITH CHECKS

You may receive checks in the mail made out to the decedent. Social security checks, pension checks and annuity checks issued after the date of death need to be returned to the sender (see pages 28 and 30). Other checks need to be deposited to the decedent's bank account. The decedent is not here to endorse the check, but you can deposit to his account by writing his bank account number on the back of the check and printing beneath it "FOR DEPOSIT ONLY." The bank will accept such an endorsement and deposit the check into the decedent's account. If the check is significant in value and/or the decedent had different accounts that are accessible to different people, then there needs to be cooperation and a sense of fair play. If not, the dollar gain may not nearly offset the emotional turmoil. Such was the case with Gail.

Gail's father made her a joint owner of his checking account to assist in paying his bills. He had macular degeneration and it was increasingly difficult for him to see. The father also had a savings account that was in his name only.

Gail's brother, Richard, had a good paying job in Miami. Even though he lived at a distance, Richard, his wife and two children always spent the spring school break holidays with his father. Gail's good cooking added to the festivities.

Winters were still another time for a visit with Richard and his family. The father enjoyed leaving the blustery Illinois winter to spend a few weeks with Richard in the warm Florida sunshine. Just before New Years, the father purchased a round trip ticket to Miami. It cost several hundred dollars. Before the departure date, the father had a heart attack and died.

Gail called the airline to cancel the ticket. They refunded the money in a check made out to her father. She deposited the check into the joint account.

As part of the probate procedure, the money in the father's savings account was divided equally between Richard and his sister. Richard wondered what happened to the money from the airline tickets. Gail explained "He paid for the tickets from the joint  account, so I deposited the money back to the joint account. "

"Well aren't you going to give me half?"

"Dad meant for me to have whatever was in that joint account.  If he wanted you to have half of the money, he would have made you joint owner as well."

Richard didn't see it that way:
"That refund was part of Dad's probate estate.  It should have been deposited to his savings  account to be divided equally between us. Are you going force me to  argue this in court?"

Gail finally agreed to split the money with Richard, but the damage was done.

Gail complains that holidays are lonely since her father died.

## LOCATE OUT OF STATE ACCOUNTS
If the decedent had out of state bank or brokerage accounts, then you might be able to locate them if they mail the decedent monthly or quarterly statements. Not all institutions do so, but all institutions are required to send out an IRS tax form 1099 each year giving the amount of interest earned on that account. Once those forms come in, you will learn the location of all of the decedent's active accounts.

# COLLECT LEGAL DOCUMENTS

As you go through the papers of the decedent you may come across documents that indicate property ownership, such as bank registers, title to motor vehicles, stock or bond certificates, insurance policies, brokerage account statements, etc. Place all evidence of ownership in a single place. You will need to contact different institutions to transfer title to the proper beneficiary. Chapter 5 explains how to identify the proper beneficiary. Chapter 6 explains how to transfer the property to that beneficiary.

## LOCATING TITLE TO THE MOTOR VEHICLE
In the state of Illinois, if monies are owed on a car, then the lender takes possession of the certificate of title until the loan is paid. If you cannot find the certificate of title, then it is either lost or monies are owed on the car and the lienholder has the title. To get information you can write to:   Office of the Secretary of State, Record Inquiry Section
408 Howlett Building, Springfield, IL   62756
They charge $5 for each Title search and $5 for each Registration search. You may first want to call them  at (217) 782-6992 to determine what information they require.

If you find there is a lien on the car then contact the lienholder and get a copy of the contract that is the basis of the loan. You may find that the car is leased and not owned by the decedent. If so,  contact the lessor and get a copy of the lease agreement. Once you have the  contract, check to see whether the decedent had life insurance as part of the agreement. If he did, then the lease is now paid in full. The next of kin or the Decedent's  Representative can send the death certificate to the leasing company with  a copy of the contract and a letter requesting that the paid contract be transferred to the beneficiary who can use the car for the remainder of the leasing period, or take title to the car, whichever option is available under the lease agreement.

# COLLECT DEEDS

Collect the deeds to all property owned by the decedent. Many people keep deeds in a safe deposit box. If you cannot find the deed in the decedent's home, then you need to determine whether he had a safe deposit box. (See the end of this Chapter for information about how to get into the safe deposit box.)

If you know that the decedent owned real property (lot, residence, condominium, cooperative, time share, etc.) but you cannot locate the deed, then contact the county recorder, in the county in which the property is located, and ask for a copy of the deed. You will need to identify the parcel of land by giving the legal description of the land or its parcel identification number. You can find this information on the last tax bill sent to the decedent. If you cannot find the last tax bill, then call the Treasurer or County Collector or Assessor for the information.

You can use the same procedure if you cannot locate the deed to property owned by the decedent in another state, namely, check with the recording department in the county where the property is located. Many states keep their land records in the court house. You can call the Clerk of the Circuit Court for information. In other states there is a separate recording department and you may need to contact the County Recorder or Registrar of Deeds.

## RESIDENTIAL LEASE

If the decedent was renting his residence, then he may have a lease agreement. It is important to locate the lease because the decedent's estate may be responsible for payments under the lease. If you cannot find a lease, then ask the landlord for a copy. If the landlord reports that there was no lease, then verify with the landlord that the decedent was on a month to month basis. You will need to work out a schedule to vacate the premises.

If a written lease is in effect, then determine the end of the lease period. If that date is more than a couple of months away, then ask the landlord whether he will agree to cancel the lease on the condition that the property is vacated in good condition. If the landlord wants to hold the estate liable for the balance of the lease, then it is prudent to have an attorney review the lease to determine what rights and responsibilities remain now that the tenant is deceased.

 LAWYER

## ONGOING BUSINESS

If the decedent had his own business or was a partner or shareholder of a small company, then the Personal Representative (or next of kin, if he died without a Will) needs to contact the company accountant to obtain the company's business records. If there is a company attorney, then contact the attorney for assistance in continuing to operate the business or terminating it. If you are a beneficiary of the estate, consider consulting with your own attorney to determine your rights and responsibilities in the business.

# COLLECT TAX RECORDS

You will need to file the decedent's final state and federal income tax return so you need to collect all of his tax records that he filed for the past 3 years. If you cannot locate his prior tax records, then check his personal telephone book and/or his personal bank register to see if he employed an accountant. If you can locate his accountant, then contact the accountant to see if he/she has a copy of those records.

If you are unable to locate the decedent's federal tax records then they can be obtained from the IRS. The IRS will send copies of the decedent's tax filings to anyone who has a *fiduciary relationship* with the decedent. The IRS considers the following people to be fiduciaries:

➢ the person named as Decedent's Representative (or executor) of the decedent's Will

➢ the successor trustee of the decedent's trust

➢ if the person died without a Will, then whoever is legally entitled to possession of the decedent's property (See Chapter 5 to learn who are the beneficiaries.)

To notify the IRS of the fiduciary capacity, you need to file Form 56: NOTICE CONCERNING FIDUCIARY RELATIONSHIP

To request the copies, file IRS Form 4506:
REQUEST FOR COPY OR TRANSCRIPT OF TAX FORM
Your accountant can file these forms for you or you can obtain the forms from the IRS by calling (800) 829-3676 or you can download them from the Internet:

 **IRS FORMS WEB SITE**
http://www.irs.gov/forms_pubs/forms.html

## STATE INCOME TAX RETURN
If you cannot locate the decedent's state income tax return you can obtain copies from the Illinois Department of Revenue. The procedure for obtaining a copy is much the same as that of the IRS. Even the form number is the same, namely Illinois form 4506.

The Department Of Revenue will provide a copy of the decedent's return to anyone in a fiduciary relationship to the decedent. If the copy of the return is being requested by someone other that the decedent's spouse, the Department may require that an Executor be appointed by the probate court before they will forward a copy of the decedent's tax records.

You can call the Illinois Department of Revenue at (800) 732-8866 and ask what information they require in order to forward form 4506 to you.

You can fax your request to (217) 782-4217 or you can write to:    Illinois Department of Revenue
P.O. Box 19001
Springfield, IL 62794-9001

# FINDING LOST/ ABANDONED PROPERTY

If the decedent was forgetful, he might have lost or abandoned property, such as a bank account, contents of a safe deposit box, a pay check, a money order, an annuity, a stock, a brokerage account, a travelers check, insurance funds, etc. In Illinois, property that is unclaimed for more than 5 years is presumed to be abandoned. For example, if money is left in a bank and there is no action on the account for 5 years then it is presumed that the account is abandoned (765 ILCS 1025/2).

Any person or institution holding abandoned property is required to turn over the property to the Illinois Department of Financial Institutions, who then publishes notice in a newspaper that the property is abandoned. If no one comes forward, all tangible property is sold at public auction and the proceeds turned over to the State Treasurer (765 ILCS 1023/12 and 1025/18). Anyone who later makes a valid claim for the property will receive the abandoned cash, or net proceeds of the sale, from the State Treasurer.

You can inquire about unclaimed property located in Illinois by calling (217) 782-6692 or by writing to:
Office of State Treasurer
Unclaimed Property Division
P.O. Box 19496
Springfield, IL   62794-9496

## CLAIMS FOR DECEDENT VICTIMS OF HOLOCAUST

The New York State Banking Department has a special Claims Processing Office for Holocaust survivors or their heirs. The office processes claims for Swiss bank accounts that were dormant since the end of World War II. You can call them at (800) 695-3318.

## CLAIMS IN OTHER STATES

Each state has an agency or department that is responsible for handling lost, abandoned or unclaimed property located within that state. If the decedent had residences in other states, then call the UNCLAIMED or ABANDONED PROPERTY department to see if the decedent has unclaimed property in that state.

 **EAGLE PUBLISHING COMPANY OF BOCA**
lists telephone numbers for the
unclaimed property division for
each state at their web site:
www.eaglepublishing.com

# LOCATE CONTRACTS

If the decedent belonged to a health club or gym, he may have prepaid for the year. Look for the club contract. It will give the terms of the agreement. If you cannot locate the contract then contact the company for a copy of the agreement. If the contract was prepaid, then determine whether the agreement provides for a refund for the unused portion.

## SERVICE CONTRACT

Many people purchase appliance service contracts to have their appliances serviced in the event that an appliance should need repair. If the decedent had a security system then he may have had a service contract with a company to monitor the system and contact the police in the event of a break-in.

If the decedent had a service contract, then you need to locate it and determine whether it can be assigned to the new owner of the property. If the contract is assignable, the new owner can reimburse the decedent's estate for the unused portion. If the contract cannot be assigned, then once the property is transferred, try to obtain a refund for the unused portion of the contract.

# LOCATE OUT OF STATE ACCOUNTS

If the decedent had out of state bank or brokerage accounts, then you might be able to locate them if they mail the decedent monthly or quarterly statements. Not all institutions do so, but all institutions are required to send out an IRS tax form 1099 each year giving the amount of interest earned on that account. Once those forms come in, you will learn the location of all of the decedent's active accounts.

# LOCATING THE WILL

Illinois law requires that the person who has the decedent's original Will must immediately file it with the Clerk of the Probate court in the county where the decedent resided. There is only one original Will, so it is important to hand carry the original document to the Clerk. If you are unable to make the delivery in person, you can mail the Will to the Clerk, but send it by registered mail so that you will have proof of delivery.  Make a copy of the Will for your own records before delivering it to  the Clerk. Once the Will is deposited with the court, the Clerk  keeps it until someone begins a probate procedure. It may be that no probate procedure is necessary, in which case the Will remains in possession of the court (755 ILCS 5/6-1, 6-7).

*Special Situation*

## WILL DRAFTED IN ANOTHER STATE OR COUNTRY

The state of Illinois respects the laws of other states and countries. If a Will is drafted in another state or country and executed according to the laws of that state or country, then it is valid in the state of Illinois (755 ILCS 5/7-4(c)).

If the Will is written in a foreign language, then it must be accompanied by a true and complete English translation before it can be admitted to Probate.

 OUT OF STATE PROPERTY

If the decedent had his residence in Illinois and owned property in another state, you may need to have a probate procedure in Illinois and an *ancillary* (secondary) probate procedure in the other state. It could be done the other way around; namely, you could have the probate in the other state and the ancillary procedure in Illinois.

If probate is to be in another state, then the original Will will need to be delivered to the Probate court in that state. The Decedent's Representative (or next of kin, if no Will) should consult with an attorney in each state to determine the best course of action. Convenience and cost are important considerations, but you also need to consider that each state has its own tax structure and probate statutes. Ask each attorney whether the location of the probate procedure will have any effect on who is to inherit the property or how much the estate will be taxed.

 OUT OF STATE RESIDENCE

If the decedent had his residence in another state, then the Will can be deposited in the county where the decedent's property is located. Before you deposit the Will, consult with an attorney experienced in Probate matters to determine whether the Will needs to be probated in Illinois or in the state of his residence. If the Will is to be probated in another state, then it is best to contact an attorney in that state and arrange to have the Will deposited with the Probate court in the state of his residence.

# THE MISSING WILL

It is estimated that 70% of the population do not have a Will, so if you cannot find a Will, chances are that the decedent did not have one. If you think that the decedent had a Will, but you cannot find it, then try to locate the decedent's check book for the past few years and see whether he paid any attorney fees. If you are able to locate the decedent's attorney, then call and inquire whether the attorney ever drafted a Will for the decedent, and if so, whether the attorney has the original Will in his possession.

If the attorney has the original Will, then ask the attorney to file the Will to the Clerk of the Circuit Court. Asking the attorney to file the Will with the court does not obligate you to employ the attorney should you later find that a formal probate procedure is necessary, nor does it obligate you to start a probate proceeding unless one is necessary.

 **LAWYER**   A COPY AND NO ORIGINAL

If you have a copy of the Will but cannot locate the original then the court will allow the estate of the decedent to be probated using the copy, provided you can prove that the document is a true copy of the decedent's valid, unrevoked Will (755 ILCS 5/6-4). You will need to employ an attorney who is experienced in probate matters to present such proof to the court.

If you believe that the decedent had a Will but you cannot find it, then check to see if the decedent had a safe deposit box. If he did, you will need to gain entry to that box to see whether the Will is in the box. See the next page for an explanation of how to gain entry to the safe deposit box.

# ACCESSING THE SAFE DEPOSIT BOX

If the decedent had a safe deposit box and he was the only person with access to the safe deposit box, then Illinois statute 755 ILCS 15/1 gives any interested party the right to go to the bank and ask the bank (or safe deposit box lessor) to allow them to examine the contents of the box.

An "interested person" is anyone of the following people:

▶ the person named as Executor of the decedent's Will

▶ the decedent's spouse

▶ the decedent's parent

▶ the decedent's adult descendant

▶ the decedent's brother or sister

If none of the above people are available, then the lessor can give access to anyone who the lessor thinks has a legitimate interest in having the decedent's Will filed with the court, or who is arranging for the decedent's burial.

The interested person can examine the contents of the box, but may not take anything from it. If the Will is in the box, the lessor can deliver it to the Clerk of the Circuit Court in the county where the decedent lived. Nothing else may be removed from the safe deposit box until someone provides proof to the bank that he/she is legally entitled to take possession of the remaining contents of the safe deposit box. See Chapter 6 (page 128) for an explanation of what type of probate procedure is necessary in order to get possession of the remaining items in the safe deposit box.

You may save much time and hassle if you call the bank ahead of time and make an appointment to meet with an officer of the bank. If you are gaining access because you are named as the Executor of the Will, then you need to bring a copy of the Will with you. Ask the bank what other identification they will require of you. Most banks require that you bring a certified copy of the death certificate, so you may need to wait until you receive the death certificate to prove to the bank officials that the owner of the box is dead.

The statute requires that the interested person give the lessor an Affidavit stating that he is an interested person and wants to examine the contents because he believes the decedent's Will is in the box. Ask the bank if they have an Affidavit form on hand. If not you can use the form on the next page.

An *Affidavit* is a written statement of facts that the *Affiant* (the person signing the document) states is true. You will need to sign the Affidavit in the presence of a Notary Public to verify that the statements made in the Affidavit are true. Most banks have a Notary Public on the premises, but you may want to verify that one will be available when you are there.

# AFFIDAVIT PURSUANT TO ILLINOIS STATUTE 755 ILCS 15/1

BEFORE ME, this day personally appeared the Affiant, who being duly sworn, says that the following information is true and correct according to his/her best knowledge and belief:

1. My name and address are:

_____

2. The decedent _____ (name)
   died on _____
   A certified copy of the death certificate is attached hereto.

3. I am interested in the filing of the lessee's will or in the arrangements for his burial.

4. I believe the box may contain the will or burial documents.

5. I am an interested person in accordance with Illinois statute.

_____
SIGNATURE OF AFFIANT


STATE OF ILLINOIS)
COUNTY OF _____)

Sworn to and subscribed before me on this day _____


_____
NOTARY PUBLIC

# What Bills Need To Be Paid?    4

If the decedent owed money, and he left money to pay those bills, then whoever settles his estate is responsible to use those monies to pay the bills. If decedent had no money in his name only because he held all his money jointly with his spouse, is the spouse responsible to use those funds to pay those debts? Years ago, the question was never asked. It was just assumed that monies owed by one, were the obligation of the other. We need to go back in history to understand the reasoning.

We inherited our court system from England. Under the old English common law, once a woman married, her legal identity merged with that of her husband. A married woman had no right to own property or to enter into a contract in her own name. Once married, a woman became totally dependent on her husband and he was legally responsible to provide her with basic necessities — food, clothing, shelter and medical services. If anyone provided these necessities to his wife, then the husband was obliged to pay for them. This law was called the **Doctrine of Necessaries**.

# THE SPOUSE'S RESPONSIBILITY

In the early 1900's many states passed laws giving married women the right to own property and to enter into a contract without her husband's permission. Once these Married Women's Rights laws were passed, a series of court cases tested whether the Doctrine of Necessaries still applied. Questions that judges had to decide were:

*If a wife can own property and contract to pay for her own necessaries, should her husband be responsible for her debts?*

*And if the husband is responsible for his wife's debts, should she be responsible for his?*

Some states answered "No" to both questions and passed laws repealing the Doctrine of Necessaries. Illinois answered "Well, maybe..."

The Illinois Rights of Married Persons Acts states:

> Neither husband or wife shall be liable for the debts or liabilities of the other incurred before marriage, and (<u>except as herein otherwise provided</u>) they shall not be liable for the separate debts of each other..."

This law seems to be saying that the Doctrine of Necessaries does not apply, but the "except as herein otherwise provided" (we underlined it for emphasis) makes it quite the opposite. Somethings included in the exception are as follows:

### PAYMENT AGREED TO IN WRITING
If the surviving spouse agreed, in writing, to pay for the debt of the decedent, then the surviving spouse remains responsible to pay for it (750 ILCS 65/15 (a)2(A).

## FAMILY EXPENSE AND CHILD'S EDUCATION

Both husband and wife are responsible to pay for the expenses of the family and for the education of the children (750 ILCS 65/15 (a)1). "Expenses of the family" is not defined in the statute but a simple example would be the case where a husband signs a lease to rent an apartment for the family to live in. If the husband dies, then the wife is responsible to continue making payments under that lease agreement regardless of whether she signed the lease agreement.

## GOODS IN POSSESSION OF THE OTHER SPOUSE

If one spouse purchases something and gives it to the other spouse, then both are equally liable to pay for the item (750 ILCS 65/15 (a)(1)(B). For example, suppose the decedent purchased a ring for his wife and put it on his credit card. If he dies, his wife must pay the charge even though the credit card was in his name only.

But suppose the decedent used his credit card to pay for his business lunches. If his spouse did not participate in those lunches and the credit card was in his name only, then the spouse is not liable to pay that debt.

## SERVICES ORDERED BY THE OTHER SPOUSE

If one spouse orders a service for the benefit of the other, then both are liable to pay for that service. This most often comes up in the context of nursing home care. Suppose the husband is ill and needs nursing care. If his wife has him admitted to a health care facility, then both are equally liable to pay for that care.

Family expenses, hospital bills, nursing home bills, legal fees, funeral expenses, all must all be paid by the surviving spouse, so in essence, the Doctrine of Necessaries remains in effect in the state of Illinois.

# IS ANYONE OTHER THAN THE SPOUSE LIABLE?

As discussed, if the spouse requested care for the decedent, then the surviving spouse is liable to pay for that care. But suppose someone other than the spouse requested the care. Is that person liable to pay for the decedent's care if the decedent died without funds?

The issue of payment most often arises in relation to services provided by nursing homes. When a person enters a nursing home, he is usually too ill to speak for himself or even sign his name. The nursing home administrator will ask a family member to sign a battery of papers on behalf of the patient before allowing the patient to enter the facility. Buried in that stack of papers may be a statement that the family member agrees to be responsible for payment to the nursing home. If the patient is single and of limited means, then the facility may refuse to admit the patient unless a family member agrees to be responsible to pay the bill.

If a nursing home accepts Medicare or Medicaid payments, then under the Federal Nursing Home Reform Law, that nursing home is prohibited from requiring a family member to guarantee payment as a condition of allowing the patient to enter that facility (USC Title 42 §1395I-3(c)(5)(A)(ii). Nonetheless, it is common practice for the nursing home, in effect, to say "Either someone agrees to pay for the patient's bill or you need to find a different facility."

Their position is understandable. Most nursing homes are business establishments and not charitable organizations. The nursing home must be paid for the services they provide or they soon will be out of business.

For an insolvent patient, the solution to the problem is to have the patient admitted to a facility as a Medicaid patient. But suppose the decedent had some money when he entered the nursing home but later died without sufficient funds to pay for his care? If you agreed to be responsible for payment only because the nursing home would not accept him without the guarantee, are you now liable to pay the decedent's final nursing home bill?

An experienced Elder Law attorney will be able to answer these questions after examining the documents that you signed and the conditions under which the patient entered the nursing home.

# JOINT DEBTS

A *joint debt* is a debt that two or more people are responsible to pay. Usually the contract or promissory note reads that both parties agree to *joint and severable* liability, meaning they both agree to pay the debt and each of them, individually, agree to be pay the debt. A joint debt can also be in some form of monies owed by one person with payment guaranteed by another person. If the person who owes the money does not pay, then the *guarantor* is responsible to pay the debt.

Before paying a bill, determine whether it is the decedent's debt or a joint debt. Hospital bills, nursing home bills, funeral expenses, legal fees incurred because of the decedent's death are all debts of the decedent's estate. They are not joint debts unless someone guaranteed payment for the monies owed.

If another person is jointly responsible for monies owed by the decedent, then that bill should be paid from any joint account held with the decedent. If the joint debtor did not have a joint account with the decedent, then the joint debtor must pay the bill from his/her own funds.

## JOINT PROPERTY BUT NO JOINT DEBT

Suppose all of the decedent's funds are held jointly with a family member and the joint owner of the account did not agree to pay those debts? Can the creditor require that half of the joint funds be set aside to pay the debt?

The answer to this question depends on how the account was set up. If a bank account is opened by two or more persons, each able to withdraw monies from the account, then the surviving owner(s) own all of the money in the account as of the date of death. The creditor has no right to any of the account funds (765 ILCS 1005/2 a).

The same applies to stocks and bonds provided they were purchased so that if one owner dies, then the survivor is the owner of that security. Usually the face of the security identifies the way the security was purchased. For example, if a stock or bond is issued in the name of two persons and the face of the security says they own the security as *joint tenants with rights of survivorship*; or if the security is issued to the two persons *or their survivor*, then should either of them die, the security belongs to the surviving owner. The decedent's creditors have no right to the security.

If two people own a security and it can be set up so that if one owner dies, then his share goes to his heirs (and not to the surviving owner). In such case, if one owner dies, his share becomes part of his estate and is available to pay his debts. The surviving owner still owns his own half and that is not available to the decedent's creditors. Securities and bank accounts that are set up in this manner are identified as *Tenants in Common.* For example, the account or security may read:
"PETER SMITH and RAYMOND WALKER AS TENANTS IN COMMON"
or "PETER SMITH and RAYMOND WALKER, T-I-C."

If the decedent held a security (or bank account) jointly with another, but no right of survivorship is stated either on the security or in the contract that established the security, then the account is considered to be a Tenancy-In-Common (765 ILCS 1005/2).

# PAYING THE DECEDENT'S BILLS

If the decedent owed money and he died owning property, belonging to him alone, such as a bank account, securities, or real property, then there may be sufficient money available to pay monies owed by the decedent. There will need to be a probate procedure so that the Decedent's Representative can gain possession of the assets and then use those assets to pay all valid debts.

Once the probate procedure begins, the Decedent's Representative will officially notify the creditors of the death and give them an opportunity to come forward and produce evidence showing the amount owed. The Representative will need to look over each unpaid invoice and decide whether it is a valid bill. The problem with making that decision is that the decedent is not here to say whether he actually received the goods and services now being billed to his estate.

That is especially the case for medical or nursing care bills. An example of improper billing brought to the attention of this author was that of a bill submitted for a physical examination of the decedent. The bill listed the date of the examination as July 10th, but the decedent died on July 9th. Other incorrect billings may not be as obvious, so each invoice needs to be carefully examined.

If the Representative decides to challenge a bill, and is unable to settle the matter with the creditor, then the probate court will decide whether the debt is valid and should be paid.

## MEDICAL BILLS COVERED BY INSURANCE

If the decedent had health insurance you may receive an invoice stamped "THIS IS NOT A BILL." This means the health care provider has submitted the bill to the decedent's health insurance company and expects to be paid by them. Even though payment is not requested, it is important that you verify that the bill is valid for two reasons:

➢  **LATER LIABILITY**

If the insurer refuses to pay the claim, the facility will seek payment from whoever is in possession of the decedent's property, and that may reduce the amount inherited by the beneficiaries.

➢  **INCREASED HEALTH CARE COSTS**

Regardless of whether the decedent was covered by a private health care insurer or Medicare, improper billing increases the cost of health insurance to all of us. Consumers pay high premiums for health coverage. We, as taxpayers, all share the cost of Medicare. If unnecessary or fraudulent billing is not checked, then ultimately, we all pay.

 *Special Situation*   MEDICARE  FRAUD

If you believe that you have come across a case of Medicare fraud, you can call the ANTI-FRAUD HOTLINE (800) 447-8477 and report the incident to the Office of the Inspector General of the United States Department of Health and Human Services.

In Illinois, you can contact the ILLINOIS DEPARTMENT ON AGING in Springfield at (800) 252-8966.

# HOW TO CHECK MEDICARE BILLING

If the decedent was covered by Medicare, then an important billing question is whether the health care provider agreed to accept Medicare *assignment of benefits*, meaning that they agreed to accept payment directly from Medicare. If so, the maximum liability for the patient is **20%** of the amount determined as reasonable by Medicare. For example, suppose a doctor bills Medicare $1,000 for medical treatment of the decedent. If Medicare determines that a reasonable fee is $800, then the patient is liable for 20% of the $800 ($160).

Health care providers who do not accept Medicare assignment bill the patient directly. They can charge up to 15% more than the amount allowed by Medicare. If the decedent knew and agreed to be liable for the payment, then his estate may be liable for whatever Medicare doesn't pay. For example, if a doctor's bill is $1,000 and Medicare allows $800, then Medicare will reimburse the decedent's estate 80% of $800 ($640). The doctor may charge the estate 15% more than the $800 ($920) and the estate may be liable for the difference: $920 - $640 or $280.

To summarize:
For health care providers accepting Medicare assignment, the most they can bill the decedent's estate is 20% of what Medicare allows (not 20% of what they bill.)

Those who do not accept Medicare assignment, can bill 15% more than the amount allowed by Medicare. The decedent's estate may be liable for the difference between the amount billed and the amount paid by Medicare.

In either case, if the decedent had secondary health care insurance, then the secondary insurer may be liable for the difference. If you have a question about billing call
MEDICARE PART B CUSTOMER SERVICE (800) 333-7586.

# DENIAL OF
# MEDICARE COVERAGE

If the health care provider reports to you that services provided to the decedent are not covered by Medicare, or if the facility submits the bill to Medicare and Medicare refuses to pay, then check to see if you agree with that  ruling by determining what services are covered under Medicare.  See page 47 of this book for information about how to obtain pamphlets that explain what medical  treatments are covered under Medicare.

If you believe that the decedent has wrongly been denied coverage, then you can appeal that decision. Call the State Health Insurance Assistance Program at (800) 548-9034 and they will explain how to appeal a denial of payment.  If you are calling from out of state, then call (217) 785-9021.  For the hearing impaired the TDD number is (217) 524-4872.

If you wish to have an attorney assist with your appeal, then call the Illinois Bar at (217) 525-5297 for a referral to an attorney experienced in Medicare appeals.  Some attorneys work *pro bono* (literally for the public good; i.e. without charge) but  most charge to assist in an appeal. Federal statute 42 U.S.C.406(a)(2)(A) limits the amount an  attorney may charge for a successful Medicare appeal to 25% of the amount recovered or $4,000, whichever is the lesser value.

# SOME THINGS ARE CREDITOR PROOF

Sometimes it happens that the decedent had money or property titled in his name only, but he also had a significant amount of debt. In such cases the beneficiaries may wonder whether they should go through a probate procedure if there will be little, if anything, left after the creditors are paid. Before making the decision consider that some assets are protected under Illinois law:

## ✧ PERSONAL PROPERTY ✧

Illinois statute (735 ILCS 5/12-1003) exempts certain personal property from the claims of creditors, meaning that a creditor cannot take those items as payment for monies owed by the debtor. Once a debtor dies, his family (spouse and children who are living with him) are entitled to that exemption. If the decedent was the head of a family, then his spouse and/or children own the following items and these items cannot be taken away to pay the decedent's debts :

⇨  clothing, family bible, school books, family pictures

⇨  other personal property worth no more than $2,000

⇨  an award under a crime victim's reparation act

⇨  payment because of a personal injury up to $7,500

⇨  The decedent's *equity interest* (value of item less monies owed on it) in a motor vehicle up to $1,200.

# ✧ THE SPOUSE'S AWARD ✧

The decedent's spouse is entitled to support for 9 months following the death. The amount is determined by the Probate court after considering the life style enjoyed by the couple prior to death and how much money there is in the estate. The minimum spousal award is $10,000. This money is exempt from any claim made by a creditor of the decedent. In fact, if the spouse dies before the award is paid in full, then the balance of the spouse's award is given to the spouse's estate (755 ILCS 5/15-1).

---

 **LAWYER**                WILL PROVIDES FOR
SUPPORT OF SPOUSE

If the decedent's Will says in effect "The money I give to my spouse in this Will is intended to be in lieu of (in place of) the Spouse's Award," then that gift can replace the Spouse's Award (755 ILCS 5/15-1(b)). There is a potential problem associated with accepting the gift. If the decedent had many debts, then those debts must be paid before any gift can be made. If the spouse agrees to accept the gift in place of the Spouse's Award, it could be that the spouse comes away with nothing after all the debts are paid. In such case, it is better to renounce the gift and ask the court to award money to support the spouse for 9 months.

The job of the Decedent's Representative is to settle the decedent's estate impartially, and without favor to any one person. If the spouse is not the Representative of the decedent's estate, and there are considerable debts, then the spouse should think about employing an attorney to represent his/her interests and that of the decedent's dependent children (if any).

---

## ✧ THE CHILD'S AWARD ✧

If the decedent had a minor or adult dependent child, then that child is entitled to support for the 9 months following the death. An adult dependent child is someone who is unable to support himself and who is likely to become a public charge.

The amount of the child's award depends on the child's life-style prior to the death, with $5,000 as the least amount of money that the court can award. The child is entitled to the award, regardless of whether the child resides with the surviving spouse. As with the spouse's award, the child's award is creditor proof (755 ILCS 5/15-2 and 25-1).

## ✧ LIFE INSURANCE PROCEEDS ✧

If the life of the decedent was insured, then the beneficiary of the policy can keep the proceeds of the policy. The decedent's creditors cannot make any claim to the proceeds of the insurance policy (735 ILCS 5/12-1001 f).

## ✧ RETIREMENT PLANS ✧

If decedent had an annuity or an Individual Retirement Account ("IRA") and the benefits of that annuity or IRA are inherited by a beneficiary (and not to the decedent's estate) then the beneficiary inherits the money from the annuity or IRA account free from the claims decedent's creditors (735 ILCS 5/12-1006).

# ✦ STATUTORY CUSTODIAL CLAIMS ✦

If during the last three years of life, the decedent was disabled, and needed to be cared for by the spouse, parent, brother, sister, or child of the decedent, then the caretaker is entitled to be paid for his/her efforts. The probate court will determine the actual amount to be paid. The court will take into account the caretaker's lost employment opportunities, lost life-style opportunities and emotional distress suffered as a result of caring for the disabled family member. The court will base the custodial award on the nature and extent of disability. Subject to the amount available in the estate, the minium amount the court will award is:  $100,000 if the decedent was 100% disabled;

$75,000 if 75% disabled;

$50,000 if 50% disabled;

$25,000 if 25% disabled.

(755 ILCS 5/18-1.1)

---

 **LAWYER**    CLAIM MUST BE FILED

The amount awarded as a custodial claim comes "right off the top" of the decedent's estate.  If there are creditors or other people who will not receive anything because of  a custodial claim, then there may be a court battle.  The job of the Representative's attorney is to see that the Representative administers the estate according to the decedent's Will (if any) and according to the laws of the state of Illinois. If you are going to make a custodial claim, and you anticipate a battle, then it is important  to employ your own attorney to protect your interests.  A custodial claim must be made in writing and filed with the court in a timely manner, so you will need to employ an attorney, just as soon after the death as you are able.

---

# ✧ THERE IS A PRIORITY OF PAYMENT ✧

Not all probate debts are equal. Illinois statute establishes an order of priority for payment of claims made against the decedent's estate (755 ILCS 5/18-10):

## CLASS 1: FUNERAL, PROBATE EXPENSES and CUSTODIAL CLAIMS

**FUNERAL and BURIAL EXPENSES:** Anyone (including the spouse) who paid for the reasonable funeral and burial expenses of the decedent is entitled to be reimbursed. Burial expenses include a marker for the burial space and care of the burial site. If these monies are not promptly paid then the person who paid for these items is entitled to interest of 9% beginning 60 days from the day the monies were due.

**EXPENSES OF ADMINISTRATION:** If a probate procedure is necessary, then all of the fees and costs must be paid. This includes filing fees, the cost of publishing notices, reasonable attorney fees and reasonable Executor fees.

**CUSTODIAL CLAIMS:** If the decedent was disabled during the last three years of his life, then his family caretaker is entitled to be paid for that care. The monies paid are free of any creditor's claim.

## CLASS 2: THE SURVIVING SPOUSE AWARD

If the decedent was married, or had minor or dependent children, then they are entitled to receive support payments for the 9 months following his death (see page 85). The spouse or guardian of the child needs to have the Decedent's Representative apply for the award as soon as the procedure begins.

## CLASS 3: MONIES DUE TO THE UNITED STATES

If the decedent owed back taxes to the IRS, or if the decedent had a school loan backed by the federal government, then these debts are 3rd in priority of payment.

## CLASS 4:  PAYROLL DEBTS

If the decedent employed workers, and owed them money for work done within the four months of his death, then they are 4th in priority of payment.  Each employee is limited to a maximum of $800 as payment in this class.  If more than $800 is due, then the employee can file a claim for the balance of the payment as a CLASS 7 debtor.

## CLASS 5:  MONIES HELD IN TRUST BY THE DECEDENT

If the decedent was holding money (or property) in trust for someone or for some business enterprise, and the trust property cannot be found, then the beneficiaries of the trust can make a claim on the decedent's estate for the missing property.  Such claims are a CLASS 5 debt.

## CLASS 6:  MONIES OWED TO THE STATE

If the decedent owed any back taxes to the state of Illinois, or if he owed property taxes to a county, township, city or village, then those funds are 6th in priority of payment.

## CLASS 7:  ALL OTHER CLAIMS

Any other debt or claim  on the estate is 7th in priority. There is no priority within the class, so if there is not sufficient money to pay all CLASS 7 debts, each will receive a pro rata share.

Illinois law requires that claims against the Probate Estate be paid in the above order.  For example, suppose the decedent was single  and left enough money to pay for his probate, the funeral, and his taxes (the first 3 classes) with $100,000 left over.  If there are no other debts then the  beneficiaries get the $100,000.  But if the decedent was married with two minor children, the spouse could  ask for support for herself and the children (Class 2). It could well be, that the support payment uses up all the money in the estate and there is nothing left to pay any other beneficiary or any creditor.

# DECEDENT
# ON MEDICAID

Medicaid is a program that provides medical and long term nursing care for people with low income and limited resources. The program is funded jointly by the federal and state government. Federal law 42 U.S.C. 1396(p) requires the state to put into effect a plan to recover monies spent from the estate of a deceased Medicaid recipient. Usually there are no monies to recover because to qualify for Medicaid, a person may have no more than $2,000 in their own name.

Sometimes it happens that a person on Medicaid dies and his estate later receives money perhaps as part of a cash settlement of a lawsuit. The state has the right to be reimbursed for government funds spent on the decedent during his lifetime. In such case, the state of Illinois becomes a Class 6 creditor, meaning that all the creditors in Class 1 through Class 5 have priority over any claim filed by the state of Illinois against the estate of the decedent.

## ✧ THERE IS A STATUTE OF LIMITATIONS ✧

Finally, consider that there is a statute of limitations for bringing a claim against the Probate Estate of the decedent. The first job of the Executor (or Administrator) is to tell the decedent's creditors that the decedent died, and that a probate procedure is in progress. If the Executor knows the identity of a creditor, then he must give the creditor notice by mail. The Executor must publish notice in a newspaper in the county where the Will is being probated, for three successive weeks to inform any unknown creditor of the death. If a creditor fails to file his claim six months after the date of the first publication, or 3 months from the date the Executor mailed notice to the creditor, then his claim is barred (755 ILCS 5/18-3).

But what if no one starts a probate procedure?
Illinois Statute (755 ILCS 18-12(b), (d)) states that if a claim is not filed within two years after the death, then that claim cannot be enforced against the estate, the Decedent's Representative, or any of the beneficiaries.

There are exceptions to the two-year limit such as mortgages and federal claims and certain liens on the decedent's property. But, in general, if no one begins a probate procedure until two years have passed, then the beneficiaries may be able to obtain possession of the decedent's assets free from creditor claims.

Read on before you decide to wait out the two years.

 **LAWYER**

## DECEDENT LEAVING CONSIDERABLE DEBT

If the decedent died leaving much debt and no property, then the solution is simple. No probate, no one gets paid. But if the decedent had property and died owing a significant amount of money, his heirs may be tempted to wait the two year period and begin probate at that time. Such a strategy may turn out to be more hassle than its worth. Some creditors are tenacious and will use whatever legal strategy is available in order to be paid. For example, a creditor can petition the court to be appointed to begin the probate procedure and administer the estate. The person named as Executor in the decedent's Will loses his right to administer the estate if he/she does not do so within 30 days of being notified of the death (755 ILCS 5/6-3).

Family members may object to having a creditor as the Representative, so there could be a court battle over who should be appointed as Representative. Once probate begins there may be additional litigation regarding which bills should be paid and in what priority.

Court battles are expensive, emotionally as well as financially. Before you decide to wait out a creditor by postponing probate for two years, consult with an attorney experienced in probate matters for his/her opinion about the best way to administer the estate.

# MONIES OWED TO THE DECEDENT

Suppose you owed money to the decedent? Do you need to pay that debt now that he is dead? That depends on whether there is some written document that says the debt is forgiven once the decedent dies. For example, suppose the decedent lent you money to buy your home. If he left a Will saying that once he dies, your debt is forgiven, then you do not need to make any more payments. If you signed a promissory note and mortgage at the time you borrowed the money from the decedent, then the Decedent's Representative should sign the original promissory note "PAID IN FULL" and return the note to you. If the mortgage was recorded, then the Decedent's Representative should sign and record a satisfaction of mortgage.

If you owed the decedent money and there is no Will, or if there is a Will, no mention of forgiving the debt, then you still owe the money. If you borrowed the money from the decedent and his spouse, then you need to pay the debt to the spouse. If you borrowed the money from the decedent only, then the debt becomes an asset to the estate of the decedent, meaning that you now owe the money to the decedent's heirs. If you are one of those heirs, you can deduct the money from your inheritance.

For example, suppose your father left $70,000 in a bank account to be divided equally between you and your two brothers. If you owed your father $20,000, then your father's estate is really worth $90,000. Instead of paying the $20,000, you can agree to receive $10,000 and have the $20,000 debt forgiven. Each of your brothers will then receive $30,000 in cash.

# Who Are The Beneficiaries? 5

A question that comes up early on is who is entitled to the property of the decedent. To answer the question you first need to know how the property was titled (owned) as of the date of death.

There are three ways to own property. The decedent could have owned property jointly with another person; or in trust for another person; or the decedent could have owned property that was titled in his name only.

In general, upon the decedent's death:

> **Joint Property** belongs to the surviving joint owner.
>
> **Trust Property** belongs to the beneficiary of the trust.
>
> Property owned by the **decedent only** belongs to beneficiaries named in the Will.
> If there is no Will, then the property goes to his heirs as per the Illinois Rules of Descent and Distribution.
>
> **NOTE** ⇨ If the decedent was married, then his spouse may have rights in his property.

This chapter explains each of these types of ownership in detail.

# PROPERTY HELD JOINTLY

Bank accounts, securities, motor vehicles, real property can all be owned jointly by two or more people. If one of the joint owners dies, then the survivor(s) continue to own their share of the property. Who owns the share belonging to the decedent depends on how the joint ownership was set up:

## THE JOINT BANK ACCOUNT

As explained in Chapter 4, if a bank account is set up in the name of two people with rights of survivorship then if one joint owner dies, the other owns all of the money in the account. The surviving owner of that account is free to withdraw all of the funds and close it out (205 ILCS 115/2).

If a joint bank account is held in three names, each with rights of survival, then when one of the joint owners dies any one of the remaining owners can withdraw all of the funds in the account. It could become a race to the bank to take out all the money. But that would only serves to cause hard feelings. With such an arrangement, the remaining owners need to cooperate with each other and come to a joint decision about how to divide the account equitably.

# JOINTLY HELD SECURITIES

The same rule applies to Illinois securities held jointly with rights of survivorship, namely, if one owner dies, then the security belongs to the remaining owners (765 ILCS 1005 (2b)). You can determine whether the decedent owns a security alone or jointly with another by examining the face of the stock or bond certificate. If two names are printed on the certificate as joint tenants, the surviving owner can either cash in the security or ask the company to issue a new certificate in the name of the surviving owner. You will need to forward a certified copy of the death certificate to the company and ask that they send you the necessary forms to make the change.

Each state has its own securities regulations. If a security held in two or more names, was registered or purchased in another state, then you will need to contact the company to determine who now owns the stock.

If the decedent held securities in a brokerage account then the name of the owner of that account is printed on the monthly or quarterly brokerage statement. Not all brokerage houses print the name of a joint owner on the brokerage statement so you need to contact the brokerage house and request a copy of the contract that is the basis of the account. It may be that the account is held jointly, or perhaps the decedent named a beneficiary who now owns the account. The contract will show when the account was opened and the terms of the brokerage account.

If you determine that the account is held jointly or for the benefit of someone, then have the brokerage firm forward the necessary forms to make the transfer to the proper owner or beneficiary.

## JOINTLY HELD MOTOR VEHICLES

If a motor vehicle is held jointly, the name of both owners is printed on the title to the motor vehicle. If one person dies, the other owns the car. To remove the decedent's name from the title all you need do is take the original title certificate and a certified copy of the death certificate to a Driver's License facility and they will assist you with the necessary paper work. The current charge to issue a new title certificate is $65. Illinois law (625 ILCS 5/3-114) requires that you do this within 120 days of the death, however, it is important to have the title to the car changed as soon as possible so that, in the event the surviving owner is in an accident, there is no question about the decedent's estate being liable for damage done.

## ILLINOIS REAL PROPERTY HELD JOINTLY

The name of the owner of real property is printed on the front page of the deed. To determine whether the decedent owned the property jointly with another, you need to look at the last recorded deed. (See page 60 if you cannot locate the deed.)

The top paragraph of the deed identifies the person who transferred the property to the current owner. That person is identified as the "Grantor." The person who is now the owner of the property is referred to as the "Grantee." For example:
"The GRANTOR, ROBERT TRAYNOR, of the city of . . .
conveys and warrants to
ALFRED CODY, SR. and ROBERT CODY, JR.
not in Tenancy in Common, but in JOINT TENANCY,
the following described Real Estate . . .

In this example Alfred and Robert are the Grantees and current owners of the property.

## 🗎 DEED HELD AS JOINT TENANTS

If the deed identifies the decedent and one or more other persons as on the previous page as:
**JOINT TENANTS, AND NOT AS TENANTS IN COMMON**
or as: **JOINT TENANTS WITH RIGHTS OF SURVIVORSHIP**
then upon the decedent's death, the surviving persons own the property. The surviving owners do not need to do anything to establish their ownership. They are free to occupy the property or sell the property.

The decedent's name remains on the deed. If you are the surviving joint owner and you wish to sell or transfer the property, you will need to give the title insurer a certified copy of the death certificate to prove that you are the sole owner. If you do not intend to sell or transfer the property in the near future, then it is adviseable to have your attorney record the death certificate along with a document called a Deceased Joint Tenancy Affidavit. The Deceased Joint Tenancy Affidavit identifies the property, giving its address, Permanent Real Estate Index Number, and the full legal description of the property.

Once these documents are recorded with the Recorder of Deeds in the county where the property is located, anyone who examines the title to the property will know that one of the joint owners died and that surviving joint tenants now own the property.

## 🗐 DEED HELD AS TENANTS IN COMMON

If the Grantee section of the deed identifies the decedent and another as TENANTS IN COMMON then the decedent's share belongs to whomever the decedent named as his beneficiary in his Will. If the decedent died without a Will, then the Illinois Rules of Descent and Distribution determine who inherits the property. See page 107 for an explanation of the law.

There is no right of survivorship unless the deed specifically says so. If a deed simply names two or more people as Grantee but does not say that they are Tenants In Common, nor does it say that there are any rights of survivorship, then that is the same as a Tenancy in Common (765 ILCS 1005/1).

 **☎ LAWYER**     THE AMBIGUOUS DEED

Most deeds clearly state whether the joint owners of the property intend a surviving owner to inherit the decedents share. But some deeds are not all that descriptive. For example, if the deed reads "JOINT TENANTS" and nothing more, then depending on the the facts surrounding the conveyance, it may be that the surviving owner does not inherit the decedent's share. If you have any question about how to interpret a deed, it is best to consult with an attorney.

## 🗐 DEED HELD AS HUSBAND AND WIFE

If the Grantee section of the deed indicates that the Grantees are married, for example:

TODD AMES AND SUSAN AMES, HIS WIFE

or

TODD AMES AND SUSAN AMES, HUSBAND AND WIFE

or

TODD AMES AND SUSAN AMES, TENANTS BY ENTIRETY

then when one spouse dies, and providing they are married at the time of death, the surviving spouse owns the property 100% even though the deed still shows the two names. The surviving spouse should have the death certificate and Deceased Joint Tenancy Affidavit recorded to establish that now there is just one owner.

---

 **LAWYER**　　　**DIVORCED PRIOR TO DEATH**

If the decedent was divorced before he died, and the deed was not changed, i.e., it still says "Husband and Wife," then unless the Final Judgment of Dissolution states otherwise, all real property held by the couple as husband and wife becomes property held as Tenants-In-Common with each person owning half the property (765 ILCS 1005/1c). The decedent's half of the property will descend to his heirs or beneficiaries and not to his former spouse. You may need the assistance of a Probate attorney to have a new deed issued that identifies the new owners of the property.

---

A *Life Estate* interest in real property means that the person who owns the Life Estate has the right to live in that property until he/she dies. While the owner of the Life Estate is alive, the Grantee has no right to occupy the property. Once the owner of the Life Estate dies, the property belongs to the person who is named as Grantee on the deed.

You can identify a Life Estate interest by examining the face of the deed. If somewhere on the face of the deed you see the phrase **RESERVING A LIFE ESTATE** to the decedent then the Grantee(s) now own the property. For example, suppose the granting paragraph of the deed reads:

THIS INDENTURE, made this day
between PETER REILLY, a single man
hereinafter referred to as "Grantor"

and, RACHEL SMITHE, a married woman,
hereinafter referred to as "Grantee"

**RESERVING A LIFE ESTATE TO THE GRANTOR**

Once Peter dies, all Rachel need do is have the death certificate recorded to establish that she now has complete ownership of the property and can occupy, lease or sell it as she sees fit.

┌─────────────────────────────────────────────┐
│  ⬡ *Special*          OUT OF STATE PROPERTY  │
│    *Situation*⟩                              │
│                                              │
│  This chapter relates only to property owned by the │
│  decedent in the state of Illinois.  If the decedent owned │
│  property in another state or country, then the laws of │
│  that state or country determine who will inherit that │
│  property and you will need to consult with an attorney │
│  in that state to determine who owns the property now │
│  that the Grantee is dead. │
└─────────────────────────────────────────────┘

 INVALID DEED

The discussion about who now owns real property left by the decedent presumes that you are in possession of the most recent valid deed. This may not be the case.  The decedent could have signed a different deed after the deed you have in your possession.

Before you come to any conclusion about who inherits the property it is advisable to have an  attorney, or a title company, do a title search to determine the owner of the property as  of the decedent's date of death.

# PROPERTY HELD IN TRUST

## BANK/ SECURITY ACCOUNTS

If a bank account is held in the name of the decedent "in trust for" or "for the benefit of" someone, then once the bank has a certified copy of the death certificate, the bank will turn over the account to the beneficiary. Sometimes such accounts are referred to as a *Totten Trust Account*. (205 ILCS 115/3). Similarly, if a security or a securities brokerage account is held "in trust for" someone, then upon receipt of the death certificate, that account becomes the property of the beneficiary.

If the bank or security account is registered in the name of the decedent "as trustee under a revocable living trust agreement," that means the decedent was the trustee of a trust and the bank will turn over that account to the Successor Trustee of the trust. Banks usually require a copy of the trust when the account was opened, so the bank probably knows the identity of the Successor Trustee. If the trust was amended to name a different Successor Trustee, you need to give the bank a copy of the amendment along with a certified copy of the death certificate.

DIVORCED PRIOR TO DEATH: If the decedent had a trust agreement and he was divorced prior to death, but neglected to change his trust, then any provision in the trust relating to the spouse, will be read as if the spouse died on the day they were divorced (760 ILCS 35/1(a)).

## MOTOR VEHICLE

If the motor vehicle is held in the name of the decedent "as trustee," then the motor vehicle is part of the trust property. The motor vehicle remains in the trust once the decedent trustee dies. The Successor Trustee will need to contact the motor vehicle bureau to have title changed to that of the Successor Trustee.

## REAL PROPERTY HELD IN TRUST

If the decedent had a trust and put property that he owned in the trust then the deed may read something like this:

**THIS INDENTURE**
made this day between
JOHN ZAMORA and MARIA ZAMORA, his wife,
hereinafter referred to as "Grantor"

and JOHN ZAMORA, **trustee of the
JOHN ZAMORA TRUST
CREATED UNDER TRUST AGREEMENT
DATED FEBRUARY 26, 1999,**
hereinafter referred to as "Grantee"

Once the trustee (John Zamora) dies then that property still remains in the trust. The trust document will say whether the person who takes John's place as trustee (the Successor Trustee ) should sell or keep the property or perhaps give it to a beneficiary.

If no instruction is given in the trust, then what the Successor Trustee does with the property may be affected by laws relating to the administration of trust property in the state where the property is located. If you are a beneficiary of the trust and you are concerned about what the Successor Trustee will do with the property, then it is best to consult with your attorney.

If the decedent owned property that was in his name only (not jointly or in trust for someone) then that property is identified as the decedent's **Probate Estate**. It is called the Probate Estate because some sort of probate procedure will be necessary before the heirs can get possession of that property. Who is entitled to the decedent's Probate Estate depends on whether the decedent died *testate* (with a Will) or *intestate* (without a Will), If the decedent died testate, then the beneficiaries of the decedent's property are identified in the Will. If a Illinois resident dies intestate, then the state of Illinois provides one for him in the form of the ILLINOIS RULES OF DESCENT AND DISTRIBUTION (755 ILCS 5/2-1). This law determines who inherits the decedent's probate estate and what percentage of the probate estate each heir is to receive once all the bills and costs associated with the probate procedure are paid.

The law recognizes the right of the family to inherit the decedent's property. The law covers all possible relationships beginning with the decedent's spouse. The term "spouse" means someone who was legally married to the decedent in the state of Illinois or elsewhere. Same sex marriages are prohibited in Illinois and such marriages are invalid even if that marriage is legal elsewhere (750 ILCS 5/213, 213.1).

---

 LAWYER    COMMON LAW SPOUSE

Common law marriages are not valid in Illinois, but if the common law marriage took place in a state or country that recognizes such marriages, then it might be that the spouse has rights in the decedent's property. You will need the counsel of an attorney to determine the intestate rights (if any) of a common law spouse (750 ILCS 5/214).

---

# RULES OF DESCENT AND DISTRIBUTION

## MARRIED, NO CHILDREN

The Illinois Rules of Descent and Distribution provides that if, at the time of death, the decedent was married and had no surviving *descendants* (children, grandchildren, great-grandchildren, etc.) then all of the decedent's probate estate goes to the surviving spouse

## MARRIED WITH CHILDREN

If the decedent was survived by descendants, all of whom are the children of the surviving spouse, then the spouse gets half of the probate estate. The other half goes to the descendants, in equal shares, *per stirpes*, meaning that if a child dies before the decedent, then the children of the deceased child divide, equally, the share intended for the deceased child.

## SINGLE WITH CHILDREN

If the decedent was unmarried at the time of his death, but had descendants, then they inherit all of his property, in equal shares, per stirpes.

## SINGLE, NO CHILDREN, AND A SURVIVING PARENT

If the decedent had no children, but he had a surviving parent and/or brother and/or sister, then his estate is divided into equal shares, one for each parent and one for each brother and sister. If one of his parents is deceased, then the surviving parent gets a double share. If a sibling (brother or sister) is deceased but with surviving children, then that share goes to the children in equal shares, per stirpes. There is no distinction for relatives of half blood, i.e., if the decedent had one brother from the same set of parents, and a sister with the same mother and a different father, then both brother and sister receive an equal share of the decedent's estate (755 ILCS 5/2.1 a, b, c, d, h).

## SURVIVING GRANDPARENT, AUNT, UNCLE OR COUSIN

If the decedent had no surviving parent, brothers, sisters, nephews or nieces, then the Probate Estate is divided in half, with half going to the decedent's next of kin on his mother's side and the other half going to the decedent's next of kin on his father's side. Illinois statute (755 ILCS 5/2-1) explains the order of distribution in detail.

## THE STATE: HEIR OF LAST RESORT

If a person dies without a Will and he has absolutely no relations then, as a last resort, his property goes to the state government. Any real property owned by the decedent becomes the property of the county where the property is located. Any personal property (bank accounts, securities, etc.) goes to the county where the decedent lived. If the decedent was not a resident of Illinois, then it goes to the county where the property is located (755 ILCS 5/2-1 (h)).

## NO SHARE FOR KILLER

If a person is convicted of intentionally and unjustifiably causing the death of the decedent, then that person forfeits all benefits with respect to the decedent's estate. In such case, regardless of whether the decedent died with or without a Will, his estate is distributed as if the killer died before the decedent. This includes property held jointly with the decedent, for example if the decedent and his killer had a joint bank account, all of the money in the account goes to the decedent's estate (755 ILCS 5/2-6).

# WHO DIED FIRST?

If a person died without a Will, who inherits property depends on who outlived the decedent. For example, if the decedent dies without a Will with one child and one grandchild, then the child gets all of his property. But suppose the father and child die together in a car crash, and no one knows who died first, how is the property distributed in that case?

According to Illinois statute, each person will be assumed to have survived the other and the property of each distributed in that manner. In the above example, the father will be assumed to have survived his son, so that means the grandchild will inherit the share intended for the son. Let's further suppose that the son had a Will that left $10,000 to his father. In that case, the father is assumed to have died first, so the $10,000 will go to whoever the son named in to Will as an alternate beneficiary of the gift.

Also suppose, that the father and son owned property jointly, then if they die simultaneously, the property is divided with one half going to the estate of the father and the other half to the estate of his son. (755 ILCS 5/3-1).

# WHAT'S A CHILD?

The Illinois Rules of Descent and Distribution are based on the parent-child relationship. Illinois has three laws that define the relationship insofar as it relates to the right of the child to inherit property of someone who died intestate:

## THE POSTHUMOUS CHILD
If a child is born to the decedent after death, then that child has the same rights as one born before his death (755 ILCS 5/2-3).

## THE ADOPTED CHILD
An adopted child has the same rights as does a natural child of the decedent, provided the child lived with and was adopted by the adoptive parent before the child reached 18 years of age. If the child was adopted after his/her 18th birthday, then the adopted person has the same rights to inherit from the adoptive parent as does a natural child, but not from the relatives of his adoptive parents. For example, if the decedent was the adoptive grandparent of someone adopted after the age of 18, then unless the grandparent left a specific gift for that adopted person in his Will, the adopted person has no right to inherit anything from the adoptive grandparent in the state of Illinois (755 ILCS 5/2-4).

---

 **LAWYER**   PERSON ADOPTED AFTER 18

The above law was adopted by the Illinois legislature in 1997 and applies to Wills drafted after 1/1/98. If the decedent's Will was signed after 1/1/98 and there is someone who was adopted after the age of 18, then it is important to consult with an attorney to determine the rights of the adopted person.

---

## NON-MARITAL CHILD

A child born out of wedlock has the same rights to inherit from his/her natural father as does one born in wedlock, provided:

☑ the decedent acknowledged the child as his own

— or —

☑ paternity is established by clear and convincing evidence

— or —

☑ paternity is established by a court
(755 ILCS 5/2-2).

---

 **LAWYER** | **DECEDENT DENIED PATERNITY**

If the decedent denied his paternity, then it will take a court procedure to establish (or disprove) paternity. If you want to establish paternity, then you will need to consult with an attorney who is experienced in litigation. If the family plans to cremate the decedent, you may need to have your attorney move quickly to bar cremation until the matter is settled.

---

**LAWYER** | **THE NEGLECTED CHILD**

If a minor or dependent child dies owning property, then under the Rules of Descent and Distribution the parents will inherit that property — but not if they neglected their parental duties. If a parent has wilfully neglected or failed to support a child for a year or more prior to the child's death, then the amount that parent can inherit may be greatly reduced, or eliminated altogether, by the Probate court (755 ILCS 5/2-6.5). You will need to employ an attorney to bring the matter before the court.

# RIGHTS OF A CHILD UNDER THE WILL

We discussed the rights of children when the parent dies without a Will, but suppose the decedent left a Will and did not include anything for a child. Is that child entitled to some part of the decedent's estate? The answer is "no," provided the decedent left a valid Will clearly stating that it was the decedent's wish not to give anything to the child.

But suppose, the decedent made no mention of the child. Perhaps the Will was made before the child was born. If the decedent made a Will and then later had a child without changing his Will to include the child, then that child has the right to inherit as much of the decedent's estate as if the decedent died intestate (755 ILCS 5/4-10).

---

 **LAWYER**     THE "FORGOTTEN" CHILD

Suppose the decedent made a Will and neglected to make any mention of that child in his Will. The child could challenge the Will arguing that the decedent simply "forgot" to include something for that child. Such challenge will probably provoke a court battle. The named beneficiaries, will no doubt argue that the decedent was estranged from the "forgotten" child, and that the omission was deliberate.

If you wish to challenge a Will on this, or any other ground, you can expect a court battle. You will need to employ an attorney experienced in litigation matters to do so.

---

# WHEN TO CHALLENGE THE WILL

If the decedent left a Will, then the Will states who is to receive the property — provided the Will is valid. In the state of Illinois for a decedent's Will to be effective and enforceable, then at the time the decedent made the Will:

➤ he was 18 years of age or older

➤ he was of sound mind meaning, he knew what he was doing (namely making a Will); what property he had, and who of his relatives would, under ordinary circumstances, expect to inherit his property.

➤ he signed the Will in the presence of at least two witnesses.

(755 ILCS 5/4-1, 4-3).

The Will must be made by a person who is not being unduly influenced by anyone. Illinois statute requires impartial witnesses to the Will. If the only witness to the Will is also a beneficiary of the Will, or the witness' spouse is a beneficiary of the Will, then the gift made in the Will is void. If such a Will is submitted to probate, it will be read and interpreted as if the gift were not made (755 ILCS 5/4-6).

If a Will is witnessed by a beneficiary and also by other, impartial, witnesses, then the Will can be admitted to probate; but the better form is to have the Will witnessed by people who have no interest in the Will.

 **LAWYER** | THE PROBLEM WILL

Sometimes, a Will is not clear or it can be read in two different ways. In such case, it is important to consult with an attorney, before deciding "who gets what."

Still another problem is a Will that is not properly witnessed. Illinois law requires at least two people testify that they witnessed the decedent sign the Will. If two witnesses signed the Will at the same time that the decedent signed the Will, then that is evidence that they saw him sign it. If the Will has one or no witness signature, then it may be that the court will declare the Will as invalid in the state of Illinois. In such case, the decedent is considered to have died intestate and his property will be distributed according to the Illinois Rules of Descent and Distribution.

The decedent may have left a Will that he wrote in his own hand, but no one witnessed him signing the Will. Such a Will is called a *holographic Will.* The problem with a holographic Will is its authenticity. Because no one saw the decedent sign the Will, it is hard to determine whether the Will was written by the decedent or is a forgery.

The state of Illinois will not accept an unwitnessed Will into probate but there are other states that will. If the decedent was a resident of another state and all he left was a holographic Will, then you should consult with an attorney to determine if the Will can be probated in that state.

Sometimes a person who is of sound mind, makes a Will, but that Will has the effect of giving a spouse or a minor child less than is required under Illinois law. One such example is that of Anne. Hers was not an easy life. She worked long hours as a waitress. She divorced her hard drinking, first husband. The final judgment gave Anne the house, the car, $28,000 in securities and sole custody of their daughter. After the divorce Anne had her attorney prepare a Will leaving all she owned to her daughter.

Some years later she met and married Harry, a chef at the restaurant where she worked. He moved into her home and they later had a son. Anne's daughter was 19, and her stepbrother 12, when Anne died after a lengthy battle with cancer. Just before she died, Anne gave $10,000 to her daughter to pay for her room and board at college. She told her daughter that she was leaving her Will as written because she knew that Harry would take good care of their son.

Anne did not own much when she died — her house, now worth $80,000, her furnishings, her car (worth $7,000) and securities worth about $20,000. The house, car and securities were titled in her Anne's name only.

When the funeral was over, Harry discovered the Will. He realized that Anne drafted the Will long before they met, but the thing that really upset him, was having his stepdaughter tell him that she intended to put the house up for sale and that he would need to find another place to live.

Harry went to his attorney.
"I was a good husband to Nancy, taking care of her right up to the end. Don't I have any rights? And what about my son — doesn't he have any rights?"

"He sure does. Illinois law provides that if a child is born after a Will is made, then that child is entitled to inherit as much as he would have inherited if his parent died intestate. If Anne died intestate, half her estate would have gone to her two children. That means  your son is entitled to 1/4th of Anne's estate (755 ILCS 5/4-10)."

"But what about the $10,000 she gave to her daughter just before she died?  Shouldn't my son get his share of that money?"

"Anne was free to make a gift of her property at any time prior to her death.  That gift does not count as part of her daughter's inheritance unless Anne signed some document saying that the gift was an advancement of her daughter's inheritance (755 ILCS 5/2-5)."

"And what about my rights?"

As for your rights, Illinois law (750 ILCS 10/4(a)(3)) allows you to *waive* (give up)  your rights in your  spouse's estate. Did you sign any pre-marital agreement giving up any or all of your rights?"

"Absolutely not!"

"In that case, you have lots of rights. Illinois law (755 ILCS 5/2-8) gives  you the right to renounce the Will that Anne wrote.  If you do, then you are entitled to one third of all of her property. You and your son might also be entitled to be paid  support from Anne's estate while probate is  being conducted. How much you receive will be up to the judge. In addition you may be entitled to a statutory claim for the nursing care you gave to your wife during the last 3 years of her life. The judge will set the amount of the award. It could be as much as $100,000.

"Sounds good to me."

"As for the homestead, even though it was in Anne's name only, Illinois law (755 ILCS 5/20-1 (b)) provides that you are entitled to continue to live in your homestead, unless Anne specifically stated in her Will that the house was to go to her daughter. "

"No, the Will said that all of her estate was to go to her daughter. Nothing was specifically said about the house."

"In that case, then unless the court finds that the house must be sold to pay Anne's debts, you can remain in the house if you want it to be included as your share of Anne's estate."

As it turned out, Harry did keep the house as part of his inheritance. The judge awarded support payments for Anne's son, but not to Harry. The judge did grant Harry's custodial claim.

There was little left for Anne's daughter after:
$$ funeral expenses       $$ attorney's fees
$$ Anne's medical bills    $$ costs of probate
$$ Harry's custodial claim and share of the inheritance
$$ support payment for Anne's son and his share of the inheritance

Things turned out very differently than Anne planned. Had she been advised about Illinois law, she could have held title to her house, car and securities jointly with her daughter. If Anne did so, then those items would not have been part of her probate estate and her daughter would have owned them upon Anne's death.

But the moral of the story, for the purpose of this discussion, is that if you believe that the decedent's Will is not valid or is not drafted according to Illinois law, then you need to consult with an attorney determine your legal rights under that Will.

# Getting Possession Of The Property

Knowing who is entitled to receive the decedent's property is one thing. Getting that property is another. As explained in the previous chapter if the property is held jointly with someone, or in a trust for someone, then the property belongs to the joint owner or beneficiary and that person can get possession of the property simply by giving a certified copy of the death certificate to the financial institution.

If the decedent held property in his name only, then a probate procedure may be necessary in order to transfer ownership to the proper beneficiary. In Illinois, probate procedures usually require the assistance of an attorney, but there are a few items that you can obtain on your own.

This chapter explains the various probate procedures and when it is appropriate to use that procedure.

# DISTRIBUTING PERSONAL PROPERTY

Too often, the first person to discover the body will help himself to the decedent's *personal effects* (clothing, jewelry, appliances, electrical equipment, cameras, books, household items and furnishing, etc.). Unless that person is the decedent's sole beneficiary, such action is unconscionable, if not illegal.

If the decedent was married and did not have children, then all of the decedent's personal effects belong to his spouse unless he left a Will giving that item of personal property to someone else. If the decedent was the head of a household, then his spouse is entitled to keep all of the personal items as described on page 84 free of any creditor claims.

If the decedent was not married, then all of his personal effects should be given to the person appointed as the Decedent's Representative. The Representative then has the duty to distribute the property according to the decedent's Will, or if the decedent died intestate, according to the Illinois Rules of Descent and Distribution.

If you find that there is no need for a Probate procedure and the decedent did not have a Will then his next of kin need to divide the personal effects among themselves in approximately equal proportions. Most personal effects have little, if any, monetary value. Furniture may be worth less than it costs to ship. In such case, the beneficiaries may decide to donate the personal property to the decedent's favorite charity.

## WHAT'S EQUAL?

The decedent's Will or if no Will, then the Illinois Rules of Descent and Distribution may direct that the decedent's personal property be divided equally between two or more beneficiaries. The problem with the term "equal" is that people have different ideas of what "equal" means. Unless there is clear evidence that the decedent's Will meant something else, "equal" refers to the monetary value of the item and not to the number of items received. For example, to divide the decedent's personal effects equally, one beneficiary may receive an expensive item of jewelry and another beneficiary may receive several items whose overall value is approximately equal to that single piece of jewelry.

When distributing personal effects there needs to be cooperation and perhaps compromise, or else bitter arguments might arise over items of little monetary value.

One such argument occurred when an elderly woman died who was rich only in her love for her five children and 12 grandchildren. After the funeral, the children gathered in their mother's apartment. Each child had his/her own furnishings and no need for anything in the apartment. They agreed to donate all of their mother's personal effects to a local charity with the exception of a few items of sentimental value.

Each child took some small item as a remembrance —
a handkerchief, a large platter that their mother used to
serve family dinners, a doily their mother crocheted.
Things went smoothly until it came to her photograph
album. Frank, the youngest sibling, said, "I'll take this."
Marie objected saying, "But there are pictures in that
album that I want."

Frank retorted, "You already took all the pictures Mom had
on her dresser."

The argument went downhill from there. Unsettled
sibling rivalries boiled over, fueled by the hurt of the loss
that they were all experiencing.

It almost came to blows when the eldest settled the
argument: "Frank you make copies of all of the photos in
the album for Marie. Marie, you make copies of all of the
pictures that you took and give them to Frank. This way
you both will have a complete set of Mom's pictures. And
while you're at it, make copies for the rest of us."

# THE SMALL ESTATE AFFIDAVIT

Suppose that the decedent had his affairs arranged so that the only thing he had in his name was a brokerage account worth $25,000. Or perhaps he had coins in a safe deposit box worth $10,000. If the total value of all of the decedent's personal property is not greater than $50,000, then the proper beneficiary can get possession of these items by giving the person who holds the property a SMALL ESTATE AFFIDAVIT. Illinois statute (755 ILCS 5/25-1) provides a form for the Affidavit. The form is printed on the next page.

To use the Small Estate Affidavit all of the following must be true:

☑ The gross value of the decedent's personal property does not exceed $50,000.

☑ No probate procedure is pending and none is necessary; in particular, there is no real property to be transferred by a probate procedure in this or any other state.

☑ All of the decedent's funeral expenses have been paid or arrangements are made for their payment.

☑ There is no known claim against the decedent's estate.

If the decedent left a Will, then you first need to file the Will with the court (see page 67) and get a certified copy of that Will to attach to the Small Estate Affidavit. You will need an Affidavit for each financial institution. For the above example, you would need one Affidavit for the brokerage company and another for the bank or safe deposit lessor. The Clerk of the Probate court will give you as many Certified copies of the Will as you need. There is a charge for the copies, so you may want to first call the Clerk to determine how much money you will need to pay.

You will also need to attach a Certified copy of the death certificate to each Affidavit. See page 24 if you need to order copies of the death certificate.

# SMALL ESTATE AFFIDAVIT

STATE OF ILLINOIS                    )
COUNTY OF _____ )

Affiant _____, being duly sworn states:


I, _____ (name of Affiant), on oath state:
1. (a) My post office address is:
_____

   (b) My residence address is:
_____

(c) I understand that, if I am an out-of-state resident, I submit myself to the jurisdiction of Illinois courts for all matters related to the preparation and use of this affidavit.   My agent for service of process in Illinois is:
NAME _____
ADDRESS_____
CITY_____
TELEPHONE (if any) _____
I understand that if no person is named above as my agent for service, or, if for any reason, service on the named person cannot be effectuated, the clerk of the circuit court of :
_____(county) (Judicial circuit) Illinois is recognized by Illinois law as my agent for service of process.

2.  The decedent's name is _____.
3.  The date of his death was _____ and
    I have attached a copy of the death certificate hereto.
4. The decedent's place of residence immediately before his death
    was _____

5. No letters of office are now outstanding on the decedent's estate and no petition for letters is contemplated or pending in Illinois or in any other jurisdiction, to my knowledge;

6. The gross value of the decedent's entire personal estate, including the value of all property passing to any party either by intestacy or under a will, does not exceed $50,000. (Here, list each asset, e.g., cash, stock, and its fair market value.);

NAME                              SPECIFIC SUM or  PROPERTY TO BE DISTRIBUTED

---

7. (a) All of the decedent's funeral expenses have been paid, or

  (b)  The amount of the decedent's unpaid funeral expenses and the name and post office address of each person entitled thereto are as follows:

NAME AND POST OFFICE ADDRESS                              AMOUNT

---

(Strike either 7(a) or 7(b)).

8. There is no known unpaid claimant or contested claim against the decedent, except as stated in paragraph 7.

9. (a) The names and places of residence of any surviving spouse, minor children and adult dependent* children of the decedent are as follows:

Name and Relationship     Place of Residence     Age of Minor Child

---

*(Note: An adult dependent child is one who is unable to maintain himself and is likely to become a public charge.)

(b) The award allowable to the surviving spouse of a decedent who was an Illinois resident is $_____ ($10,000 plus $5000 multiplied by the number of minor children and adult dependent children who resided with the surviving spouse at the time of the decedent's death. If any such child did not reside with the surviving spouse at the time of the decedent's death, so indicate.

(c) If there is no surviving spouse, the award allowable to the minor children and adult dependent children of a decedent who was an Illinois resident is $_____ ($10,000, plus $5,000 multiplied by the number of minor children and adult dependent children), to be divided among them in equal shares.

(Continued on next page)

10. (a) The decedent left no will. The names, places of residence and relationships of the decedent's heirs, and the portion of the estate to which each heir is entitled under the law where decedent died intestate are as follows:

Name, relationship          Age of minor    Portion of
and place of residence                        Estate

_____

OR

(b) The decedent left a will, which has been filed with the clerk of the appropriate court. A certified copy of the will on file is attached. To the best of my knowledge and belief the will on file is the decedent's last will and was signed by the decedent and the attesting witnesses as required by law and would be admittable to probate. The names and places of the residence of the legatees and the portion of the estate, if any, to which each legatee is entitled are as follows:

Name, relationship          Age of minor    Portion of
and place of residence                        Estate

_____

(Strike either (a) or (b)).

(c) Affiant is unaware of any dispute or potential conflict as to the heirship or will of the decedent.

11. The property described in paragraph 6 of this affidavit should be distributed as follows:

Name                 Specific Sum or Property to be Distributed

_____

The foregoing statement is made under penalty of perjury*

_____
                      Signature of Affiant

*(Note: A fraudulent statement made under penalties of perjury is perjury, as defined in Section 32-2 of the Criminal Code of 1961.)

Subscribed and sworn to before me this date _____

_____
                      Notary Public
                      Seal

## Paragraph 1.  IDENTITY OF AFFIANT

The Affiant should be the main beneficiary of the property to be transferred.  If there are two children as sole beneficiaries, then it is best if both sign as the Affiant.  Notice that a beneficiary who lives out of state can transfer the property, provided  they agree to be bound by the laws of Illinois insofar as any transfer relating to this Affidavit.

## PARAGRAPH 8:  IDENTITY OF CREDITORS

You need to identify all of the decedent's creditors (See Chapter 4).  You need to make provision to pay any valid debt from the  proceeds of the money you receive.  If there are more debts than money,  then consult with an attorney before using this Affidavit.

## Paragraph 10.  IDENTITY OF BENEFICIARIES

See Chapter 5 for a discussion of who is to inherit the decedent's property.  If there is any question in your mind, then it is best to consult with an attorney before attempting to take possession of the decedent's property.

## CAUTION     YOUR LIABILITY

If you use this Affidavit, then you are personally liable to anyone who had a right to the decedent's money.  For example, if the decedent owed money on a credit card, and you neglected to pay that debt — or if some relative was entitled to receive a share of the money, and you did not give them their proper share.  In such cases, the person who had a right to the property,  can sue you personally for the amount of money you received using the Affidavit. If they win, you will need to return the money AND  you will need to pay their attorney's fees (755 ILCS 5/25-1 (e)).

# HOW TO GET THE CONTENTS
# OF THE SAFE DEPOSIT BOX

If the decedent leased a safe deposit box together with another person, each with full authority to enter the box, then the co-lessee of the box can remove all of its contents. If, however, the decedent and another, both needed to be present in order to access the box, or if the decedent was the sole lessee of a safe deposit box, then some sort of probate procedure is necessary in order to get possession of the contents of the box.

If there is a full probate procedure the Decedent's Representative will be appointed by the Probate court. The court will give Letters to the Representative saying that the Representative has full authority to take possession of all of the assets that belonged to the decedent. If the decedent had a safe deposit box, then the Personal Representative can present the Letters to the bank or safe deposit box lessor, and they will give the Representative access to the box and all of its contents.

If the decedent's property is being transferred by means of a Small Estate Affidavit, then the Affidavit can be presented to the lessor of the safe deposit box. To prepare the Affidavit you will need to identify the contents of the box. See page 70 for information about how to obtain an inventory of the contents of the safe deposit box. If you are not the sole beneficiary, then all of the adult beneficiaries identified under Paragraph 11 of the Affidavit should appoint you as their agent to take the contents of the box. They can do so by signing a document that says "We appoint (name)_____ to act as our agent under the attached Small Estate Affidavit, to take possession of the contents of the decedent's safe deposit box" (755 ILCS 5/25-1 (c)).

# INCOME TAX REFUNDS

As explained in Chapter 2, you need to file the decedent's final state and federal income tax return. The returns are due by the date on which the returns would have been due had the death not occurred (IRS Reg. 1.6072-1(a)). If there is a federal refund due to the decedent and you are entitled to that money as the beneficiary of the decedent, then you can obtain the refund by filing IRS form 1310 along with the 1040. You can obtain this form 1310 from the decedent's accountant. If the decedent did not have an accountant and you wish to file yourself, then call the IRS at (800) 829-3676 to obtain the proper form. You can get instructions, forms and publications from the IRS Web site:

 INTERNAL REVENUE SERVICE WEB SITE
IRS FORMS AND INSTRUCTIONS
http://www.irs.ustreas.gov/prod/forms_pubs/forms.html

IRS PUBLICATIONS
http://www.irs.ustreas.gov/prod/forms_pubs/pubs.html

If are appointed by the Probate court as the Decedent's Representative, then you do not need to file form 1310 because once you file the decedent's final income tax return, any refund will be forwarded to you as the Representative. Similarly, a surviving spouse does not need to file form 1310 because the spouse will automatically receive any refund due on their joint return.

# TRANSFERRING THE CAR

If the decedent owned a motor vehicle then title to the car needs to be transferred to the new owner and the car registered in the state where it is going to be used. It is a good idea to limit the use of the car until it is transferred to the beneficiary. If the decedent's car is involved in an accident before the car is transferred to the new owner, then the decedent's estate may be liable for the damage. Having adequate insurance on the car may save the estate from monetary loss, but a pending lawsuit could delay the probate procedure and prevent any money from being distributed to the beneficiaries until the lawsuit is settled.

Illinois law requires that the owner of a motor vehicle be insured for at least $40,000 for bodily injury to more than one person in an accident and $15,000 property damage. Before making the transfer, have the new owner show proof of insurance. Once the transfer is made, contact the decedent's insurance company and arrange to have the decedent's motor vehicle policy cancelled. The company should refund any unused premium to the estate of the decedent.

## WHO IS ENTITLED TO THE MOTOR VEHICLE

As explained in chapter 5, if the decedent held the car jointly with another, then the joint owner now owns the car. The surviving owner should contact the local Driver's License facility and remove the decedent's name from the title (see page 98).

If the decedent owned the car with another as tenants in common, then the decedent's half goes to whomever he named in his Will. If he died intestate, then his half goes to his next of kin as determined in the Illinois Rules of Descent and Distribution (see page 107).

## CAR IN DECEDENT'S NAME ONLY

If the decedent owned the car in his name only and he was survived by a spouse or child who was living with him, then the spouse (or child) owns up to $1,200 of the value of the car (see page 84). If the decedent made a gift of his car in his Will, then the beneficiary of the car needs to pay that $1,200 to the spouse (or child).

If the decedent was not survived by a spouse or by a child, then he was free to leave his car to whomever he wished. If the decedent did not make a specific gift of the car in his Will then the car goes to the *residuary beneficiaries* under his Will, i.e. to those people who inherit whatever is left after all gifts specified in the Will are made, and all of the bills and costs of probate are paid. If the decedent did not have a Will, then the car belongs to the decedent's heirs as determined by the Rules of Descent and Distribution.

## MORE THAN ONE BENEFICIARY

If there is more than one person who has the right to inherit the car, then the beneficiaries need to decide who will take title to the car. The person who takes title to the car may need to compensate the other heirs for their share of the car. If so, then they all need to come to an agreement as to the value of the car.

# DETERMINING THE VALUE OF THE CAR

Cars are valued in many different ways. The *collateral* value of the car is the value that banks use to evaluate the car for purposes of making a loan to the owner of the car. Because banks print these values in book form, the collateral value is also referred to as the *book value* of the car. If you were to trade in a car for the purpose of purchasing a new car, then the car dealer will offer you the *wholesale* value of the car. Were you to purchase that same car from a car dealer, then he will price it at its *retail* or *fair market value*. Usually the retail price is highest, wholesale is lowest and the book value of the car is somewhere in between.

You can call your local bank to get the book value of the car. It may be more difficult to obtain the wholesale value of the car because the amount of money a dealer is willing to pay for the car depends on the value of the new car that you are purchasing. You can get some idea of the car's retail value by looking at comparable used car advertisements in the local newspaper.

 You can determine both wholesale and retail values of the car by using one or more of the search engines on the Internet to find web sites that will give both wholesale and retail car values.

If there is going to be a Probate procedure, then the Decedent's Representative will make transfer title to the car as part of that procedure. The Letters issued by the court will give the Representative authority to transfer title to the proper beneficiary.

If no probate procedure is necessary, then you can transfer title by using the Small Estate Affidavit (form RT OPR-31.13) issued by the Secretary of State of Illinois. You can obtain the form at your local Driver's License Facility or you can call the office of the Secretary of State (217) 782-6306 and they will mail you a copy. You can make the transfer by taking the Affidavit and the car title to any local Driver's License Facility. See page 59 if you cannot locate the title to the car.

You might save time by first calling the Driver's License Facility to determine what other documents they require to make the transfer and how much money it will cost.

## TRANSFERRING THE MOBILE HOME

A mobile home is a motor vehicle, so the methods described can be used to transfer the decedent's mobile home. Before transferring the motor vehicle, you need to find out whether the land on which the mobile home is located was leased or owned by the decedent.

If the decedent was renting space in a trailer park, then you need to contact the trailer park owner to transfer the lease to the beneficiary of the mobile home. If the decedent owned the land under the mobile home, then a probate procedure will be necessary to transfer the land to the proper beneficiary. See page 135 for information about transferring real property.

## Special Situation  ▷ TRANSFERRING THE LEASED CAR

The leased car is a not an asset of the estate because the decedent did not own the car.  The leased car is a liability to the estate because the decedent was obligated to pay the balance of the monies owed on the lease agreement.  The Decedent's Representative, or next of kin, needs to work out an agreement with the company to either assign the lease to a beneficiary or family member who will  agree to pay for the lease — or to have the estate pay off the lease by purchasing the car under the  terms of the lease agreement.

If the remaining  payments exceed the current market value of the car, there may be a temptation to hand the keys over to the leasing company. This may not be the best strategy,  because the leasing company can then sell the car and then sue the estate for the balance of the monies owed. If the decedent had no assets or if the only assets he had are  creditor proof, then simply returning the car may be an  option.  But if the decedent's estate has assets available to pay the balance of the lease payments, then the Decedent's Representative needs to arrange to have the car transferred  in a way that releases the estate from all further liability.

# TRANSFERRING REAL PROPERTY

To transfer real property owned by the decedent some document needs to be recorded that identifies the beneficiary, and new owner, of the property. If there is going to be a full probate procedure, then the Decedent's Representative will transfer the real property as part of the probate procedure. If the decedent's estate is worth $50,000 or less, then the property can be transferred by means of an informal probate procedure called Summary Administration:

## SUMMARY ADMINISTRATION

Summary Administration is a probate procedure designed to assist people in obtaining their inheritance in an expedited manner where the estate is small and there are no unusual circumstances. Specifically, the law allows a Summary Administration if all of the following are true:

➤ The value of *all* of the property (both real and personal property) to be transferred in the state of Illinois does not exceed $50,000.

➤ There are no unpaid claims or all monies owed by the estate are known to the beneficiaries of the estate.

➤ There are no unpaid state or federal taxes, or all provision has been made to pay the taxes.

➤ No one is entitled to a surviving spouse's or child's award, or if they are so entitled, the provision has been made for the minimum amount allowed by law.

➤ All beneficiaries have consented, in writing, to the distribution of the estate by means of a Summary Administration (755 ILCS 5/9-8).

A petition must be filed asking the Probate court to order the distribution of the assets to the proper beneficiaries. The court will set a hearing to determine if Summary Administration is appropriate. Prior to the hearing the person who files the petition must publish notice for three successive weeks in a newspaper that is published in the county where the probate is being conducted. The notice must give the decedent's date of death and tell when and where the hearing will be held.

To make sure that all of the decedent's bills are paid, the law requires that all of the beneficiaries be bonded. That means they must take out a bond equal to the amount each will receive. If it happens that a beneficiary must return his inheritance to pay any valid claim against the estate, and he refuses, then the bond can be used to make payment. But that doesn't mean that the beneficiary is off the hook. He can be personally sued by the bonding company to return the money, and if he loses, he will be required to pay his attorney's fees as well as the other person's attorney fees (755 ILCS 5/9-8).

You can pick up the Petition for Summary Administration form in the office of the Clerk of the Probate court. The Clerk is not authorized to assist you in completing the forms, so if you need assistance, you need to consult with an attorney who is experienced in Probate matters.

# THE FULL PROBATE PROCEDURE

If the decedent left real property or assets worth more than $50,000, then there needs to be a full Probate Administration.   The procedure can take anywhere from 6 months to more than a year depending on the size and complexity of the Probate Estate. It is the Decedent's Representative's job to use the Probate Estate to pay all valid claims and then to distribute what is left to the proper beneficiary.

All of the decedent's debts are paid from the Probate Estate and not from Decedent's Representative's pocket; but if the Decedent's Representative makes a mistake then he may be responsible to pay for that mistake. For example, if the Decedent's Representative pays a debt that did not need to be paid — or if the Decedent's Representative transfers property to the beneficiaries too quickly and there were still taxes due on the estate, then he may be responsible  to pay for his error.

The Decedent's Representative needs to employ an attorney to guide him through the process. It then becomes the job of the attorney for the Decedent's Representative to see to it that the estate is administered properly and without any personal liability to the Representative. The attorney has the right to  charge reasonable fees and to charge those fees to the decedent's Estate (755 ILCS 5/27-1). The attorney can  either charge a flat fee as a percentage of the estate or he can charge on an hourly basis.  Hourly fees can run anywhere from $175 an hour to $300 an hour depending on the complexity of the case.

# APPOINTING THE REPRESENTATIVE

The first step in the Probate procedure is to have someone appointed by the court as the Decedent's Representative. If there is a Will, the court will appoint the person named as Executor of the Will. If the decedent died intestate, then anyone with priority can file a *petition* (a request to the court) to be appointed, or have someone of their choice appointed, as the Representative (see page 27). If someone has the same or a higher priority, then the person seeking appointment must mail a copy of the petition to each such person. Anyone with the same or a higher priority then has the right to challenge or accept the appointment (755 ILCS 5/6-2).

Illinois law is designed to speed administration and reduce costs by allowing the Decedent's Representative the right to act independently and without court supervision. This is called an *Independent Administration*. The court will allow an Independent Administration unless the decedent's Will specifically requests that the Administration be supervised, or if the court finds that a beneficiary's interest is not adequately being protected, as may be the case with a minor or disabled beneficiary.

If the court allows an Independent Administration then the Representative can do all of the following without asking the court for permission to do so:
⇨ take possession of the estate
⇨ sell, lease or mortgage any of the estate property
⇨ borrow money on behalf of the decedent's estate
⇨ continue the decedent's business
⇨ settle claims against the decedent's estate
⇨ employ agents, accountants, attorneys
⇨ invest money of the estate
(755 ILCS 5/28-8).

## CAUTION — BENEFICIARY WHO IS NOT DECEDENT'S REPRESENTATIVE

If the court allows an Independent Administration, then the Decedent's Representative is required to send notice to each beneficiary that he/she is appointed to act independently, and to give the beneficiary a form that can be used to object to the Independent Administration (755 ILCS 5/28-2).

Allowing the Representative to act independently can save the estate money, but the downside is that without court supervision the Decedent's Representative can do some serious mischief. If you are concerned about the ability of the Decedent's Representative to properly administer the estate, then do not hesitate to fill out the form objecting to an Independent Administration and return it to the court. The court will then either grant your request for a supervised administration or will hold a hearing on the matter and then rule on your request.

# YOUR RIGHTS AS A BENEFICIARY

If you are the beneficiary of an estate, then you have many rights. First and foremost you have the right to be kept informed as to the progress of the Probate procedure. As discussed, you have the right to be notified of the appointment of a Representative and whether he can act independently or with court supervision.

### ✧ RIGHT TO YOUR OWN ATTORNEY

The attorney who handles the estate is employed by and represents the Decedent's Representative. If the estate is sizeable, then you might consider employing your own attorney to check that things are done properly and in a timely manner. If you are not in a financial position to employ an attorney, then you can take the following steps to protect you interests:

### ✧ RIGHT TO A COPY OF THE WILL

If there is a Will then you have the right to receive a copy of that Will. Once the Representative is appointed have him or his attorney forward the copy to you.

### ✧ RIGHT TO PETITION THE COURT

If an Independent Administration is being conducted, then you have the right, at any time, to petition (ask) the court to conduct a hearing on any matter that is troubling you (755 ILCS 5/28-5). If a Supervised Administration is being conducted, then you still have a right to go before the court if you believe something is seriously wrong, however, you may want to consult with an attorney prior to doing so.

## ❖ RIGHT TO COPY OF INVENTORY

If the probate is being conducted with court supervision, then the Decedent's Representative must file an inventory of all of the assets of the Probate estate within 60 days of his appointment. You can request that he give you a copy of the inventory as soon as it is filed with the court (755 ILCS 5/14-1).

If there is an Independent Administration, then the Independent Representative does not need to file the inventory with the court, but if he is bonded, he is required to give the company that issued the bond (the *surety*) a copy of the inventory within 90 days. If you give the Representative a written request for a copy of the inventory, then he must give you a copy as well (755 ILCS 5/28-6).

## ❖ RIGHT TO KNOW FEES

The Decedent's Representative is entitled to a reasonable fee. If the Representative is also a beneficiary of the estate he may decide not to take a fee and just take his inheritance. The reason may be economic. Any fee he takes is taxable as ordinary income, but monies inherited are not taxable to him as a beneficiary. Ask the Representative to tell you, in writing, whether he intends to charge a fee, and if so, how much (755 ILCS 5/27-1).

Ask the Representative to tell you how much he agreed to pay to his attorney. If he employed the attorney on an hourly basis, then ask the attorney to give you a written estimate of the time he expects to spend on the probate procedure.

If you think either of these fees are unreasonable, then you have the right to negotiate a reduction of fees. If you cannot come to an agreement, then you can petition the court to set the fees (755 ILCS 5/28-11 (9)).

### ✧ RIGHT TO AN ACCOUNTING

Before the estate is closed, the Decedent's Representative must give each residuary beneficiary an accounting, starting with the inventory value of the estate and ending with the amount of money that will be left to distribute after all the bills have been paid. The court will not require an accounting if all of the beneficiaries sign a waiver giving up their right to an accounting. If you want to know how the estate monies were spent, then you should not sign any document giving up this right (755 ILCS 5/24-1 and 5/28-6).

### ✧ RIGHT TO COPIES OF TAX RETURNS

It is important that you receive copies of all tax returns that the Decedent's Representative is obliged to file. If the Decedent's Representative fails to file a return, or fails to pay taxes, or if he under-reports a tax obligation, then you could later be called on to pay estate taxes out of the proceeds that you receive.

## ✧   IT'S YOUR RIGHT - DON'T BE INTIMIDATED

You may feel uncomfortable being assertive with a friend or family member who is Decedent's Representative. Don't be. It's your money and your legal right to be kept informed. Be especially firm if the Representative waives you off with:

"You've known me for years. Surely you trust me."

People who are trustworthy, don't ask to be trusted. They do what is right. The very fact that the Decedent's Representative is refusing to give you information is a red flag. In such cases you can explain that it is not a matter of trust, but a matter of what is your legal right.

At the same time, keep things in perspective. Your family relationship may be more important, than the money you inherit. The job of Personal Representative is often complex and demanding. If the Personal Representative is getting the job done, then let him know that you appreciate his efforts.

## THE CHECK LIST

We have discussed many things that need to be done when someone dies in the state of Illinois. There is a check list on the opposite page that you may find helpful.

You can check those items that you need to do, and then cross them off the list once they are done. We made the list as comprehensive as possible, so many items may not apply in your case. In such case, you can cross them off the list or mark them *N/A* (not applicable).

## *Things to do*

## FUNERAL ARRANGEMENTS TO BE MADE
☐ AUTOPSY ☐ ANATOMICAL GIFT
☐ DISPOSITION OF BODY OR ASHES

## DEATH CERTIFICATE
☐ RECORD WITH COUNTY RECORDER
GIVE COPY TO: _____

_____

## NOTICE OF DEATH
PEOPLE TO BE NOTIFIED _____

COMPANIES TO NOTIFY
☐ TELEPHONE COMPANY
   ☐ LOCAL CARRIER ☐ LONG DISTANCE ☐ CELLULAR
☐ NEWSPAPER (OBITUARY PRINTED)
☐ NEWSPAPER CANCELLED ☐ deposit refund
☐ SOCIAL SECURITY
☐ INTERNET SERVER
☐ TELEVISION CABLE COMPANY
☐ BASE POWER & LIGHT ☐ deposit refund
☐ POST OFFICE
☐ OTHER UTILITIES (GAS, WATER) ☐ deposit refund
☐ PENSION PLAN
☐ ANNUITY
☐ HEALTH INSURANCE COMPANY
☐ LIFE INSURANCE COMPANY
☐ HOME INSURANCE COMPANY
☐ MOTOR VEHICLE INSURANCE COMPANY
☐ CONDOMINIUM OR HOMEOWNER ASSOCIATION
☐ CANCEL SERVICE CONTRACT ☐ deposit refund
☐ CREDIT CARD COMPANIES _____

_____

_____

## *Things to do*

## REMOVE DECEDENT AS BENEFICIARY OF:

- ☐ WILL
- ☐ INSURANCE POLICY
- ☐ PENSION PLAN
- ☐ BANK OR IRA ACCOUNT
- ☐ SECURITY

## DEBTS

PAY DECEDENT'S DEBTS  (AMOUNT & CREDITOR)

_____

COLLECT MONIES OWED TO DECEDENT (AMOUNT & DEBTOR)

_____

## TAXES

- ☐ FILE FINAL FEDERAL INCOME TAX RETURN
- ☐ FILE FINAL STATE INCOME TAX RETURN
- ☐ RECEIVE INCOME TAX REFUND
- ☐ FILE ESTATE TAX RETURN

## PROPERTY TO BE TRANSFERRED

- ☐ PERSONAL EFFECTS
- ☐ MOTOR VEHICLE
- ☐ BANK ACCOUNT
- ☐ CREDIT UNION ACCOUNT
- ☐ IRA ACCOUNT
- ☐ SECURITIES
- ☐ BROKERAGE ACCOUNT
- ☐ INSURANCE PROCEEDS
- ☐ HOMESTEAD
- ☐ TIME SHARE
- ☐ OTHER REAL PROPERTY
- ☐ CONTENTS OF SAFE DEPOSIT BOX

## OTHER THINGS TO DO

_____

_____

_____

# *Preneed Arrangements* 7

Death is a wake-up call because once someone close to us dies we are reminded of our own mortality. We realize that death can be put off, but the inevitable is inevitable. Although we cannot change the fact of our death, we have the power to control the circumstances of our death by making preneed arrangements.

You can make preneed arrangements so that you will be buried in the manner you wish and where you wish. You can also make arrangements that direct the kind of medical treatments you want to be given in the event you become seriously ill.

You can legally appoint someone to make your medical decisions in the event that you are too ill to speak for yourself. If you let that person know how you feel about life support systems, autopsies and anatomical gifts then that person will be authorized to act on your behalf and will see to it that your wishes are carried out.

As this chapter will show, it is relatively simple and inexpensive to make such preneed arrangements.

# MAKING BURIAL ARRANGEMENTS

When making burial arrangements for the decedent, you may decide to purchase one or more burial spaces nearby for other family members.

If the decedent was buried in the family plot, then this is the time to take inventory of the number of spaces left and who in the family expects to use those spaces.

If all of the spaces are taken and if you plan to be cremated, then some cemeteries will allow an urn to be placed in an occupied family plot. You can call the cemetery and ask them to explain their policy as it relates to the burial of urns in currently occupied grave sites.

If you do not wish to have your cremains buried, then you can reserve a space for them in a columbarium located within the cemetery.

If you wish to have your cremains scattered then you need to let your next of kin know where and how this is to be done.

| Special Situation | VETERAN OR VETERAN'S SPOUSE |

If you are an honorably discharged veteran, you have the right to be buried in a Veterans National Cemetery. You cannot reserve a grave site in advance. If your Veteran spouse was buried in a Veterans National Cemetery then you have the right to be buried in that same grave site unless soil conditions require a separate grave site.

If you wish to be buried in a Veterans National Cemetery, then check on current availability (see page 16 for telephone numbers). Let your next of kin know your choice of cemetery.

To establish your eligibility your next of kin will need to provide the following information:

➤ the veteran's rank, serial, social security and VA claim numbers

➤ the branch of service; the date and place of entry into and separation from the service

The next of kin will also need to provide the VA with a copy of the veteran's official military discharge document bearing an official seal or a DD 214 form.

If you wish to be buried in a national cemetery, then make all of these items readily accessible to your family.

# MAKING FUNERAL ARRANGEMENTS

If you are financially able, in addition to purchasing a burial space, consider purchasing a Preneed Funeral plan. It will be easier on your family emotionally and financially if you make your own funeral arrangements. If you do not have sufficient cash on hand for the kind of funeral you desire, then many funeral directors offer an installment payment plan.

Once you decide on a plan, the funeral director will present you with a contract. The print may be small, but it is worth your effort to read it before signing. If the contract is written in "legalese" then either consult with your attorney before signing it or ask as many questions of the funeral director as is necessary to make the terms of the contract clear to you.

If you are not satisfied with the way a certain section of the contract is written then add an addendum to the contract that explains, in plain English, your understanding of that passage. If you are concerned about something that is not mentioned in the contract, then insist that the contract be amended to include that item.

In particular check to see whether the contract answers the following questions.

## Does the contract cover all costs?

The contract should contain an itemized list stating exactly what goods and services are included in the sales price. Ask the funeral director whether there will be any additional cost when you die. For example, if you have not purchased a burial space, then that cost needs to be factored in. Some funeral directors offer combination funeral and burial plans, namely contracts that include the cost of a burial space. Other contracts are for the funeral only. If you made provision for a burial space, then you need to make the funeral director aware of where you have arranged to be buried. If you have not made such provision, then the funeral director can assist you in making burial arrangements.

## Is the price guaranteed?

Some Preneed plans have a fixed price for the goods and services you chose. You are guaranteed that the goods and services will be provided upon your death, regardless of when you finally die. Other contracts do not guarantee that the price will be the same. The price for the goods and services that you have chosen under those contracts are not fixed, and the company can charge additional monies upon your death.

Illinois law requires that the contract you sign, state in capital letters, whether the price is guaranteed, or whether the monies you have paid are simply a deposit for the goods and services that you have chosen (225 ILCS 45/1a-1(a)(3)).

*How are your contract funds protected?*

Illinois laws are designed to protect the purchaser of a Preneed Funeral Plan. According to Illinois law, funeral firms are required to protect funds paid by the consumer of a Preneed Funeral Plan either by having the monies placed into a trust, or by having the funeral firm purchase a life insurance policy or an annuity to cover the funds paid by the purchaser (225 ILCS 45/1a-1(f)).

Check to see if your Preneed contract states how your monies will be protected. If the contract is silent on the issue, then have the funeral director explain how the funeral firm will guarantee your plan. If the funds are protected by being placed in a trust or escrow account, then have the funeral firm agree to furnish you with proof of the deposit once the contract is signed. Illinois law requires that the trust funds be deposited within 30 days of receipt (225 ILCS 45/2). Have the funeral firm promise, in writing, to notify you should they decide to change banks.

*Is the funeral firm reputable?*

Of course all of these safeguards may fail if you are not doing business with a reputable funeral firm. It is prudent to take the time to call the investigation division of the Illinois Department of Professional Regulation at (217) 785-0800. Ask if the funeral firm is licensed and whether any complaints have been filed against them.

## Can you cancel the contract?

If you purchased the Preneed contract in your home, or in a place other than the funeral establishment, then you have a three day "cooling off" period. This means that you have three days after signing the agreement to cancel the Preneed contract and receive all of your money back (255 ILCS 45/1a-1(b)). Illinois law also provides that once you have paid for the contract, you have the right to cancel it and receive your money back. If your monies were held in trust, then the funeral firm must return your monies plus any interest earned on the account. If your monies were placed in an insurance policy or annuity, then you will receive the cash surrender value of the policy (225 ILCS 45/4(c)). You may want to verify that your Preneed contract reflects Illinois law.

Illinois statute allows an *irrevocable* contract (one that can't be cancelled) to be sold to people who are applying for, or receiving, Medicaid, Supplemental Security Income ("SSI") or other public assistance program. Such programs place limits on the amount of assets owned by an applicant. Illinois law allows irrevocable contracts to be sold to people in these programs so as not to have the funeral contract affect their eligibility to qualify for the program (225 ILCS 45/4 (a)). If you purchase a contract and then later need to apply for any of these programs you can have the funeral firm change the contract to one that is irrevocable.

## What if you die in another state or country?

It is a good idea to have the contract spell out what provision will be made in the event that you move to another state or in the event you happen to die in another state or country. Many funeral firms are part of a national funeral service corporation with funeral firms located throughout the United States, so this is not usually a problem.

## Can the plan be changed?

Illinois statue states that you can cancel your contract and receive all of your money back, but what if your heirs need to change the plan you have chosen because:

➢ your body is missing or cannot be recovered
➢ you were buried by another facility because your heirs were unaware of your Preneed contract
➢ you died in another country and were buried there.

In any case where the funeral goods or services are provided by another firm, Illinois statute requires that all of the Preneed funds be given to your heirs, with the exception of 10% of the monies paid, or $300, whichever is the smaller amount (225 ILCS 45/4 (c)).

But what if your heirs decide on a plan different than the one you purchased? Funeral firms generally allow heirs to make changes to the plan you paid for such as:

➢ purchasing a more expensive plan and paying the difference
➢ changing to a lesser plan and receive a refund.

You might want to check whether the contract offered by the funeral firm addresses the issue of making changes to the contract after your death.

You may wonder why anyone would think of changing the decedent's funeral plan, but consider that in today's market, it is not uncommon for a Preneed contract to cost several thousand dollars. A top end funeral complete with solid bronze casket can cost upwards of $40,000.

And there may be other motivations. Consider the case of Mona, a difficult woman with a personality that can only be described as "sour." Her husband deserted her after four years of marriage leaving her to raise their son, Lester, by herself. Once Lester was grown, Mona made it clear to him that she had done her job and now he was on his own. Lester could have used some help. He married and had three children. One of his children suffered with asthma and it was a constant struggle to keep up with the medical bills.

Mona believed in being good to herself. She did not intend to, nor did she, leave much money when she died. She knew that Lester would not be able to afford a "proper" burial for her, so she purchased a funeral plan and paid close to $15,000 for it. She was pleased when the funeral director told her that the monies would be kept safely in a local bank until the time they were needed.

Lester was not familiar with Illinois law, so when Mona died he asked an attorney at the Legal Aid office to determine whether the Preneed contract was revocable.
It was.
You know the ending to this story.

If you are concerned that you get the exact type of funeral that you want, with no changes, then you might consider purchasing a life insurance policy payable to your estate with instructions in your Will that you want a court supervised administration and that the money from this policy is to be used to purchase the type of funeral you wish as directed in your Will. This ensures that no one can revoke your instructions, because the distribution of the insurance funds to the funeral firm is court supervised. It may be some time before your Will is probated so you need to give a copy of the Will to the funeral firm to be sure they carry out your wishes.

# PURCHASING BURIAL INSURANCE

Many insurance companies have specific burial insurance policies, so you might investigate such insurance plans. The cost of the policy might be less than purchasing a Preneed plan. You could insure yourself with sufficient monies to cover the cost of the burial and other miscellaneous expenses such as paying for a dinner after the burial, or paying the airfare for a family member to attend the service.

If you wish to purchase burial insurance, but you do not want to trigger a probate procedure for a single insurance policy, then you could name a trusted family member as the beneficiary of the policy. It is important that the person who is to receive the insurance funds clearly understands why he/she is named as beneficiary of the policy. It is equally important that the beneficiary agree to use the monies for the intended purpose. It isn't so much that a family member is not trustworthy as it is that they may not understand what you intended — especially in those cases where other funds are available to pay for the funeral. Too often insurance funds are left to a sibling who then refuses to contribute to the cost of the funeral saying in effect "Dad wanted me to have this money — that's why he left it to me."

To avoid a misunderstanding, put it in writing. It need not be a formal contract. It could be something as simple as a letter to the insurance beneficiary, with copies to your next of kin, saying something like:

Dear Romita,

I purchased a $10,000 insurance policy today naming you as beneficiary of the policy. As we discussed this money is to be used to pay for the following:
- my funeral and grave site
- my headstone
- perpetual care for my grave
- airfare for each of my grandchildren to attend the funeral
- dinner for the family after the wake
- lunch for the family after the funeral

If there is any money left over, please accept it as my thanks for all the effort spent on my behalf.
Love,
  Dad

P.S. I am sending a copy of this letter to your brother so that he will know that all arrangements have been made.

Whether or not you arrange to pay for your burial or funeral, you need to let your next of kin know your feelings about the burial procedure. Let your family know whether you wish to be cremated or buried. If you wish to have a religious service, then let your family know the type of service and where it is to be held. Let the family know where you wish to be buried, or if you intend to be cremated, then where to place the ashes.

## AUTOPSIES

As discussed in Chapter 1, some autopsies are optional. If you have strong feelings about allowing an optional autopsy or not allowing the procedure, then let your family know how you feel.

## ANATOMICAL GIFTS

If you wish to make an anatomical gift, you can make that donation by completing a donor card or by letting your family know that you wish to make a donation of some or all of your body parts. Donor cards are available at your local Driver's License Facility.

If you are aged, and in poor health, the local Organ Procurement Organization will probably not consider your body for transplantation of body parts, but you can still donate your body for education and research. If you wish to make such as donation, call or write to either University mentioned on page 6. They will forward a Dedication Form to you along with information on the subject. As discussed in Chapter 1, there may be a significant charge to your estate to make the donation, so you need to be aware of the cost before you decide to make the gift.

If you do not wish to make an anatomical gift, then let your family know how you feel. Of course, there are problems with just telling someone how you feel about your burial arrangements, autopsies, and anatomical gifts:

### YOU TELL THE WRONG PERSON

The person you confide in may not be present when the arrangements are made. For example, if you tell your spouse what arrangements to make then he/she may die before you do — or you could die simultaneously in a car or plane crash.

You may tell someone who does not have authority to carry out your wishes. That was the case with James. Once his wife died, he moved to a retirement community where he lived for 15 years until his death. James had two sons who lived in different states. Although he loved his sons, he had difficulty talking to either of them about serious matters. It was easier for him to talk with his friends in the retirement community. They often spoke about dying and how they felt about different burial arrangements. James would reminisce about his youth and growing up in a farming community in the plains state of Kansas. "I was happy and free. Out there you had room to breathe. It would be nice to be buried there — peaceful and spacious."

When he died, his friends told his sons about their father's desire to be buried in Kansas. They met the suggestion with scepticism and pragmatism:
"Dad didn't say anything like that to me."
"It would cost us double to arrange for burial in another state. I'm sure he didn't have that kind of expense in mind."

## THE PERSON DOES NOT CARRY OUT YOUR WISHES

The person you tell may not understand what you said or perhaps they hear only what they want to hear. An example that comes to mind is the mother who constantly complained that she felt like a burden to her children. She would often say "When I die, burn my body and throw my ashes out to sea." Her children paid no attention. When she died she was given a full funeral and buried in a local cemetery. They never asked, nor did they consider, that their mother might really have wanted to be cremated.

## WHO WANTS TO TALK ABOUT IT?

For many people the main problem with telling someone what to do when you die is talking about your death. It may be an uncomfortable, if not unpleasant, subject for you to bring up, and for your family to discuss. If this is the case, then consider putting the information in writing and give the instructions to the person who will have the job of carrying out your wishes.

You can legally appoint someone to carry out your wishes relating to the care of your person, both before and after death, by signing a document called *Powers of Attorney for Health Care*. Illinois statute contains a statutory form that you can use to appoint a Health Care Agent to carry out the wishes you express in the Powers of Attorney. The statutory form contains a *Living Will* that tells your Health Care Agent whether you do (or do not) want life support systems to be used in the event that you are dying and there is no hope for your recovery. You can look up the statutory form of the Powers of Attorney for Health Care (755 ILCS 45/4-10) by going to the nearest public library or courthouse library. You can also download the form from the Internet:

ILLINOIS STATUTES
http://www.legis.state.il.us/

If you do not appoint someone to act as your Health Care Agent and you are too sick to make your own medical decisions, then the person with priority to make your medical decisions is set by Illinois statute (755 ILCS 40/25)

1st Health Care Agent appointed under
    a Power of Attorney for Health Care
2nd A court appointed guardian of the person
3rd The spouse          4th An adult child
5th Either parent of the patient
6th Any adult brother or sister
7th Any adult grandchild    8th A close friend
9th A court appointed guardian of person's estate

A person with priority must be reasonably available, willing and competent to act. If not, the next one with priority will make the decision.

If this order of priority is not as you wish, or if there is someone you wish to exclude altogether from making your health care decisions, then it is important to sign a Power of Attorneyfor Health Care and appoint the person of your choice to act as your Health Care Agent. If not, life decisions made for you, may not be as you would have wished.

George is a case in point. His wife became ill with Alzheimer's disease. He cared for her at home for as long as he was able, but finally, it was too much for him. He placed her in a local nursing facility. He and his two daughters would visit her regularly though she barely recognized them. George met Emily at the nursing home. Her husband also suffered from Alzheimer's disease and was at the same facility. After visiting with their respective spouses they would go to the local coffee shop. One thing led to another, and soon they were an item. George's daughters were not happy with the coupling. They criticized everything about Emily, from the way she dressed to her table manners.

When Emily moved in with George, his daughters made cutting remarks about Emily's moral character. Emily didn't take it personally. She believed the girls were more concerned about their inheritance than George's happiness. A second marriage might cut into what they already considered to be rightfully theirs.

Not that George and Emily planned to wed. They both loved their respective spouses and had no intention of trying to obtain a divorce. Their understanding was that if and when they both were single, they would discuss marriage at that time.

George and Emily enjoyed each other, feeling and acting like a couple of teenagers; but their happiness was short-lived. George suffered a stroke while driving a car. His injuries from the accident combined with the severity of the stroke made for a bleak prognosis. The doctors said George would die unless they put him on a ventilator and inserted a feeding tube. Even with these life support systems, they doubted that he would come out of the coma.

Emily pleaded to keep him alive. "Let's try everything. If he doesn't improve we can always discontinue the life support systems later." George's daughters did not see it that way. "Why torture him with needles and tubes? Let him pass on peacefully."

George never signed a Living Will so no one knew whether he would want life support systems to be applied. He never appointed anyone to be his Health Care Agent to make his medical decisions in the event he was unable to do so. In the absence of a Power of Attorney for Health Care, the doctors had no choice. Under Illinois law, the daughters were 4th in priority. Emily was 8th.

George died.

# Everyman's Estate Plan

The first six chapters of this book describe how to wind up the affairs of the decedent.  As you read those chapters, you learned about the kinds of problems that can occur when someone dies.  It is relatively simple for you to make an estate plan so that your family members are not burdened with similar problems.  An *estate plan* is the arranging of one's finances to reduce (if not eliminate) probate costs and estate taxes, so that your beneficiaries inherit your property quickly and at little cost.

If you think that only wealthy people need to  prepare an estate plan, you are mistaken. Each year, heirs of relatively modest estates, spend thousands of dollars to settle an estate.  A bit of planning could have eliminated most, if not all, of the hassle and cost suffered by those families.

The suggestions in this chapter are designed to assist the average person in preparing a practical and inexpensive estate plan, so we have named this chapter EVERYMAN'S ESTATE PLAN.   Once you create your own estate plan, you can rest assured that your family will not be left with more problems than happy memories of  you.

# AVOIDING PROBATE

Probate procedures can be costly and time consuming. If you have a small estate and only one or two beneficiaries, then it is not all that difficult to arrange your finances so that there will be no need for probate when you die.

# BANK ACCOUNTS

You can arrange to have all of your bank accounts, including certificates of deposit, titled so that the money goes directly to your heirs when you die. For example, suppose all you have is a bank account with a balance of $50,000 and you want to have this go to your son and daughter when you die.  You might think that a simple solution is to put each child's name on the account, but first consider the ramifications of a joint account:

## THE JOINT ACCOUNT
A joint bank account gives each joint owner of the account complete access to that account.  If you hold the account jointly with your children, then each child can write a check on that account, the same as yourself.  When you die the remaining joint owner  (or joint owners) can withdraw all of the money from the account.  There are some potential problems with this arrangement:

### ⊠ POTENTIAL LIABILITY

If you hold a bank account jointly with one of your adult children and that child is sued or gets a divorce then the child may need to disclose their ownership of the joint account. In such a case, you may find yourself spending money to prove that the account was established for convenience only and that all of the money in that account really belongs to you.

### ⊠ OVERREACHING

If you set up a joint account with your child so that the child has authority to withdraw funds from the account, then funds may be withdrawn without your authorization. If you open a joint account with two of your children, then after your death the first child to the bank may decide to withdraw all of the money and that will, at the very least, cause hard feelings between them.

### ⊠ THE MINOR CHILD

Illinois law allows a minor to own a savings or checking account either in their own name or jointly with another (205 ILCS 105/4-7 and 115/2). But if you elect a minor as the joint owner of your account, would you want the child to have the ability to remove money from your account. If you die, would you want the minor to be able to go to the bank and withdraw all of the money?

Because of these inherent problems, you might want to hold the funds so that your beneficiary does not gain access to the monies until and unless you die. There are two ways to do so: the "pay-on-death account" and the "in trust for" account.

# THE "IN TRUST FOR" ACCOUNT

You can direct a financial institution to hold your account *in trust for* one or more beneficiaries that you name. This is also referred to as a Totten Trust account. The beneficiary does not have access to that account during your lifetime so an IN TRUST FOR account does not have the potential problem of the joint account, but it does have its Achilles' heel.

In the state of Illinois, if a person sets up a Revocable Trust then any money he/she puts into that trust can be used to pay debts that he/she may owe either before and after death. If you set up an "IN TRUST FOR" account and you owe money, when you die then your creditors may say to the bank that you were really holding that money in that account as trustee of a Revocable Trust. On that basis your creditors might ask the bank to give them the money in the account as payment for your debts.

The bank will not want to get in the middle of an argument between your creditors and the beneficiary of that account so the bank will ask a probate court to settle the argument. If the purpose of setting up an "IN TRUST FOR" account was to avoid probate, then this may not be the best approach for someone who owes significant amounts of money.

There is a simple solution to the problem of ensuring your heirs get the money in your bank account without going through probate and that is to open a "PAY-ON-DEATH" account.

# THE "PAY-ON -DEATH" ACCOUNT

The PAY-ON-DEATH ("POD") account eliminates the inherent problems of the joint account because the beneficiary does not own any part of the account until the owner of the account dies. Specifically:

⇨    The beneficiary does not have access to the account until the owner of the account dies.

⇨    During his lifetime the owner of the account is free to change beneficiaries without asking the beneficiary's permission to do so.

⇨    The owner of the account is free to add to or withdraw from the account without the knowledge or consent of the beneficiary (205 ILCS 625/4).

You can open an account with PAY-ON-DEATH instructions to the bank to give the money to your child when you die, and if the child dies before you, then to your grandchildren in equal shares, per stirpes. For example:

ELDON CONNERS POD RICHARD CONNORS LDPS

which is short-hand for:

"ELDON CONNORS owner of the account. Pay on death to RICHARD CONNORS or if he dies first, then give it to his lineal descendants in equal shares, per stirpes."

If you wish you can hold a POD account in your name only or jointly with another (815 ILCS 10/10). If you are married, you and your spouse can purchase a certificate of deposit ("CD") with a Pay-On-Death designation so once both of you have died your named beneficiary will immediately own that CD. For example:

MARY REILLY and ROBERT REILLY, JT TEN
POD ANNE HENDERSON

# TRANSFERRING SECURITIES

You can hold a stock, or bond, or a securities brokerage account jointly with another, but with the same problems as described previously. Happily, there is a statute for securities similar to the PAY-ON-DEATH statute for banks. You can instruct the holder of the security to transfer the security to a named beneficiary once you die. You can use the POD designation or you can use a TRANSFER ON DEATH ("TOD") designation. The law governing TOD accounts are the same as those of the POD account:

⇨ The beneficiary does not have access to the security until the owner dies. The owner of the security is free to change beneficiaries without asking the beneficiary's permission to do so. (815 ILCS 10/5 & 6).

Of course, if you wish you can hold the security jointly. The same laws apply with a TOD designation as with the POD designation:

⇨ If one joint owner dies, the other owns the security outright. The surviving owner has the right to change the beneficiary of the security.

⇨ If no beneficiary survives the owner, then the security goes to the estate of the last owner of the account to die.

⇨ If there are two or more beneficiaries, then they inherit the security as tenants-in-common with each owning an equal share (815 ILCS 10/2 & 7).

# GIFT FOR THE MINOR

At the beginning of this chapter, we identified three problems with a joint account: potential liability if the joint owner is sued; overreaching by the joint owner, and holding an account jointly with a minor. The POD, TOD and Totten Trust account each solve the problem of potential liability and overreaching, but if the beneficiary of such account is a minor, there still is the problem of allowing a child access to a significant amount of money.

For property located in this state, the problem is solved by applying the ILLINOIS UNIFORM TRANSFERS TO MINORS ACT. The law gives the owner of a bank account the right to name a person or a financial institution to be custodian of an account in the event that the owner dies before the beneficiary of the account reaches 21. For example:

**Patricia Barry POD Friendly Bank**
**As CUSTODIAN for Frank Barry, Jr. under the**
**ILLINOIS UNIFORM TRANSFERS TO MINORS ACT.**

Patricia is free to add or withdraw from the account during her lifetime. Once she dies, whatever remains in the account will be given to the bank as custodian. If Frank is 21 or older, the bank will give him the money. If he is not yet 21, the bank will hold the money for him until his 21st birthday. The bank can deliver or spend as much of the money for Frank's care as they think advisable. If there is a disagreement about using the funds, then Frank's parent or guardian (or Frank himself if he is 14 or older) can ask a court to order that the bank use monies for Frank's care.

The same law can be used to transfer securities, life insurance policies, even real property to a minor. The custodian does have the right to charge a reasonable fee for their efforts, so you need to check with the custodian to find out how they intend to handle the funds and the estimated cost of doing so (760 ILCS 20/10, 13, 15, 16 ).

 **LAWYER** TRANSFERRING A BUSINESS

If you own a business, be it a sole proprietorship, partnership or corporation, you need to make provision for the orderly transfer of your business interest in the event you die suddenly. An attorney who is experienced in business law (corporation, banking, bankruptcy, commercial law, franchise law, etc.) can offer suggestions as to the best method of ensuring that the business continues its operation, or terminates in an orderly fashion — whichever is applicable in your case.

If you cannot afford to employ an attorney at this time, then consult with your accountant. Let your accountant know who is to have access to your business records in the event of your incapacity or death. Discuss how company debts will be paid and how best to distribute the company assets to your heirs, in case of your death. If it is your intent that the business continue in your absence, you might consider purchasing key man insurance on your life to compensate the company for any loss suffered because of your absence. See page 44 for an explanation of key man insurance.

# REAL PROPERTY

As explained in Chapter 5, if you own real property together with another, then who will own the property upon your death depends on how the Grantee is identified on the face of the deed. If you compare the Grantee clause of the deed to the examples on pages 98 through 103 you can determine who will inherit that property should you die. If you are not satisfied with the way the property will be inherited, then you need to consult with an attorney to change the deed so that it will conform to your wishes.

If you own the property in your name only, then once you die, there will need to be a probate procedure to determine the proper beneficiary of that parcel of land. If your main objective is to avoid probate, then you can have an attorney change the deed so that once you die, the property descends to your beneficiary without the need for probate. As with bank and securities accounts there are different ways to do so, each with its own advantages and disadvantages.

## JOINT OWNERSHIP
You can have your deed changed so that you and a beneficiary are joint tenants (owners) of the property. If you do so you will avoid probate of the property but you will not be able to sell that property during your lifetime without the beneficiary's permission. And if the beneficiary gives permission and the property is sold, the beneficiary will have the legal right to half of the proceeds of the sale.

If the property is your homestead, still another disadvantage is the loss of part of your homestead tax exemption. If the beneficiary does not live in the home with you, then once you change the deed to joint ownership you will lose half of your homestead tax exemption.

# CAUTION    GIFT OF HOMESTEAD

Some people think it a good idea to simply transfer their homestead to their children to avoid probate, but continue to live there. But this just creates a new set of problems:

## ☒ RISK OF LOSS

If you transfer your homestead to a beneficiary it could be lost if the beneficiary runs into serious financial difficulties or gets sued. This is especially a risk if your child is a professional (doctor, nurse, accountant, financial planner, attorney, etc.). If your child is found to be personally liable for damages, then the house could become part of the settlement of that law suit.

If your child is (or gets) married, then this complicates matters even more so. If the child gets divorced, the property will certainly be included as part of the settlement agreement. This may be to your child's detriment because the child may need to share the value of the property with his ex-spouse. If you do not transfer the property, then it cannot become part of the marital equation.

## ☒ POSSIBLE LOSS OF GOVERNMENT BENEFITS

If you transfer property, then depending upon the value of the transfer, you could be disqualified from receiving Medicaid or Supplemental Security Income ("SSI") benefits for up to 3 years from the date of transfer. The federal and state rules that determine the period of ineligibility are complex. If nursing care may be an issue in the future, then it is best to consult with an Elder Law attorney to prepare a Medicaid Estate Plan.

## ⊠ LOSS OF HOMESTEAD TAX EXEMPTION

If you put the deed in the beneficiary's name and that property is your homestead, then unless the beneficiary lives in the homestead with you, he/she is not entitled to a homestead tax exemption. If you are eligible for a general Homestead exemption or a special exemption because you are a Disabled Veteran or Senior Citizen it will cost you more money in taxes to continue to live in your own home (35 ILCS 200/15-175).

You can avoid losing your homestead tax exemption by transferring the property to a beneficiary and keeping a LIFE ESTATE for yourself. But, as with joint ownership you will not be able to sell the property during your lifetime without the permission of all of the people you named as Grantee on the deed; and if you sell the property each Grantee is entitled to some portion of the proceeds of the sale.

## OTHER TAX CONCERNS

Before you make a real estate transfer be it joint interest, life estate or outright gift, you need to consider the tax consequences of the transfer:

☒   POSSIBLE CAPITAL GAINS TAX

If you gift your homestead to your child and continue to live there until you die, then when the child sells the property there might be a capital gains tax. The child will be taxed on the increase in value from the day <u>you</u> bought the property.

If you don't transfer your home and the child inherits the property, he/she inherits it at the market value as of your date of death. The child can sell the property at that time without any tax consequence.

☒   POSSIBLE GIFT TAX

If the value of the transfer is worth more than $10,000 you need to file a gift tax return. For most of us, this is not a problem because no gift tax needs to be paid unless the value of the property (plus the value of all gifts in excess of $10,000 that you gave over your lifetime) exceed the estate tax credit (see the schedule on page 36). But if you are in that tax bracket, then you need to be aware that you are "using up" your tax credit.

 **LAWYER** OUT OF STATE PROPERTY

Each state is in charge of the way property located in that state is transferred. If you own property in another state (or country) then you need to consult with an attorney in that state (or country) to determine how that property will be transferred to your beneficiaries once you die. Most state laws are similar to Illinois, namely, property held as **JOINT TENANTS WITH RIGHTS OF SURVIVORSHIP** or a **LIFE ESTATE INTEREST** goes to your beneficiary without the need for probate.

If you own property in another state in your name only, or as a **TENANT IN COMMON,** or if you hold property jointly with your spouse in a community property state, then a probate procedure will probably need to be held in that state. If it is necessary for your heirs to have probate procedure in Illinois, then they will need an ancillary (secondary) procedure in the state in which the property is located. This may have the effect of doubling the cost of probate to your heirs.

Still another problem is the matter of taxes. The Illinois Estate taxes are tied to the Federal Estate tax. If your estate is too small to pay Federal Estate taxes then you pay no Illinois Estate tax. This may not be the case with other states, so in addition to paying extra for the second probate procedure, your heirs may need to pay inheritance taxes in the state where the property is located. In such cases, you may wish to consult with an attorney for suggestions about how to set up your estate plan to avoid these problems.

# A TRUST MAY BE THE SOLUTION (or not)

As we have seen, many of the ways to avoid probate involve methods with undesirable trade-offs. One way to avoid some of these potential problems is to set up a trust. You may have heard this suggestion from your financial planner or attorney, or accountant. Even people of modest means are being encouraged by these professionals to use a trust as the basis of their estate plan. But trusts have their pros and cons. But before getting into that, let's first discuss what a trust is and how it works:

## SETTING UP A TRUST

To create a trust, an attorney prepares the trust document in accordance with the client's needs and desires. We will refer to the person who signs the document is referred to as the *Trustor.* That person can also be referred to as the *Grantor* or *Settlor* of the Trust. The trust document identifies who is to be the Trustee (caretaker) of property placed in the trust. Usually the Trustor appoints himself as Trustee so that he is in total control of property that he places into the trust. The trust also names a Successor Trustee who will take over the management of the trust property should the Trustor become disabled or die.

Once the trust document is properly signed, the Trustor transfers property into the trust. He does this by changing the name on the account from that of his individual name to his name as Trustee. For example, if ELAINE RICHARDS sets up a trust naming herself as trustee, and she wishes to place her bank account into the trust then all she need do is instruct the bank to change the name on the account from ELAINE RICHARDS to ELAINE RICHARDS, TRUSTEE of the ELAINE RICHARDS TRUST. Once the change is made, all the money in the bank account becomes trust property. Elaine (wearing her trustee hat) still has total control of the account, taking money out, and putting money in, as she sees fit.

The trust document states how the trust property is to be managed during Elaine's lifetime. If the trust is a Revocable Living Trust, then it will say that Elaine has the power to terminate the trust at any time and have all trust property returned to her. Should Elaine become disabled or die, then her Successor Trustee will take possession of the trust funds and manage (or distribute them) according the to direction Elaine gave in the trust document. If the trust says that once Elaine dies, the property is to be given to her beneficiary, then the Successor Trustee will do so; and in most cases without a probate procedure. If the trust directs the Successor Trustee to hold property in trust to care for a member of the Elaine's family, then the Successor Trustee will do so.

## THE GOOD PART
Setting up a trust has many good features.

### ☆ AVOID GUARDIANSHIP PROCEDURES
If you become disabled or too aged to handle your finances, then you do not need to worry about who takes care of your finances. Your trust appoints a Successor Trustee to take over the care of your trust if you are unable to do so. If you do not have a trust and you become incapacitated, a court may need to appoint a guardian to care for your property. The cost to establish and maintain the guardianship is charged to you. Guardianship procedures are expensive and once established cannot be terminated unless you die or are restored to health.

### ☆ PRIVACY
Your trust is a private document. No one but your trustee and your beneficiaries need ever read it. If you leave property in a Will and there is a probate procedure, the Will is filed with the court. The Will becomes a public document. All can see who you did (or did not) provide for in your Will.

## ☆ AVOID PROBATE

Probate procedures can be very expensive. Both the Decedent's Representative and his attorney are entitled to reasonable fees. It may be necessary to hire accountants and appraisers, as well. If you have property in two states, then two probate procedures may be necessary (one in each state) and that could be costly. If the trust is properly drafted and your property placed into the trust, you may be able to avoid probate altogether.

## ☆ CARE FOR A CHILD OR FAMILY MEMBER:

If you make provision in your trust to care the finances of a child or a family member after you die, then your Successor Trustee can do so. If your family member is immature or a born spender, you can set up a Spendthrift Trust to protect him/her from squandering the inheritance. You can direct your Successor Trustee to use trust funds to pay for the family member's health care, education or living expenses, and nothing more.

## ☆ TAX SAVINGS:

There can be substantial Estate tax savings if you are married and you and your spouse each set up your own trust. For example, suppose you and your spouse together have an estate worth one million dollars. You can each set up your own trust with $500,000. Each trust can provide that if one of you dies, the surviving spouse can use the income from the deceased partner's trust for living expenses. Once the second partner dies, all of the monies in the two trusts can be distributed, with no estate taxes due on either trust. By doing this, you each take advantage of your own Estate and Gift Tax Exclusion. If you don't separate the funds, then if one of you dies the surviving spouse has all of the money with only one deduction. For example, if the Exclusion amount is $675,000 and Estate tax rate is 37%, then the beneficiaries will pay over $120,000 in Estate taxes.

# THE PROBLEMS

A trust is an excellent estate planning tool, but there are some things you need to consider:

## ☒ COMPLEXITY

A trust is a fairly complex document, often 20 pages long. It needs to be that long because you are establishing a vehicle for taking care of your property during your lifetime, as well as after your death. The trust usually is written in "legalese," so it may take you considerable time and effort to understand it. It is important to have your trust document prepared by an attorney who has the patience to work with you until you fully understand each paragraph of the document and are satisfied that this is what you want.

## ☒ COST

Because of the thoroughness of the document and the fact that it is custom designed for you, a trust will cost much more to draft than a simple Will. In addition to the initial cost of the trust, it can be expensive to maintain the trust should you become disabled or die. Your Successor Trustee has the right to charge for his duties as trustee, as well as to charge for any specialized services performed. For example, if you choose an attorney to be Successor Trustee, then the attorney has the right to charge to manage the trust, and also charge for any legal work he performs. A financial institution can charge to serve as Successor Trustee, and also charge to manage the trust portfolio (760 ILCS 5/7).

These charges can be considerable. Before appointing someone as Successor Trustee, you need to investigate what the Successor Trustee will charge to manage the trust.

## ☒   NO CREDITOR PROTECTION

Because property held in a Revocable Living Trust is freely accessible to the Trustor, it is likewise accessible to his creditors both before and after the Trustor's death. If the Trustor dies owing money then the trust funds can be used to pay for those debts.

## ☒   TAXES MAY STILL BE A PROBLEM:

While the Trustor is operating the trust as Trustee, all of the property held in a Revocable Living Trust is taxed as if the Trustor were holding that property in his/her own name. If the value of the trust property exceeds the Estate and Gift Tax Exclusion amount (see page 36 for the value), then unless the Trustor takes some other, more advanced, Estate Planning strategy, taxes will be due and owing once the Trustor dies.

## ☒   PROBATE MIGHT STILL BE NECESSARY

The trust only works for those items that you place in the trust. If you have property that is held jointly with another, then when you die, that property will go to the joint owner and not to the trust. If you purchase a security in your name only, and forget to put it in your trust, there will need to be a probate procedure to determine the beneficiary of that security.

# MAYBE PROBATE ISN'T ALL THAT BAD

As explained, if you hold all of your property in trust or jointly with another, you may be able to avoid probate and have your property go directly to your heirs. But you may have reason not to choose either of these methods. Maybe you don't have money at this time to pay an attorney to set up a trust.

Perhaps you do not want to hold your money jointly with anyone because you are concerned about losing your independence or maybe you are concerned about keeping your money secure. Still another concern may be that if the joint owner is married then the spouse of the joint owner may have a right to some portion of that joint account according to the laws of the state where they live.

Still another reason for not holding property jointly is to be sure that your property is distributed in the way that you wish and according to the directions in your Will. If you want your money to go to several charities or to a minor child, then you may decide that it is better to make a Will rather than hold money jointly with just verbal instructions to your beneficiary about how you want the funds distributed when you die.

For example, if you hold all of your property jointly with your child, then the child is the legal owner of your property as of your date of death. If you tell your child to use some of that money for your grandchild's education, then that puts an unreasonable burden on your child because you were not specific as to exactly how much of that joint account was to be used for the child's education. Also you did not say how to use the money. Is the money for tuition only? Can the money be used to pay the child's living expenses?

Even if you give your child specific instructions about how the money is to be spent, and even if your child is honorable and with the best intentions, it may be that your grandchild gets none of the money, because your child is sued or falls upon hard times and is forced to use that money to pay debts. If you keep your property in your own name and leave a Will giving a certain amount of money for your grandchild, then he/she will know exactly how much money you left and the purpose of that gift.

If your grandchild is a minor at the time you make your Will you can appoint someone in your Will to be a custodian of the child's gift under The Illinois Uniform Transfers to Minor's Act. As discussed at the beginning of this chapter, the custodian can be a person (such as the child's parent) or trust company or financial institution. When the child reaches the age of 21, the custodian will transfer the property to the child.

If you have a Will, and hold all of your money in your name only, then you can guarantee that your property will be distributed according to the directions you give in your Will, provided you specify that the probate of your Will is to be supervised by the court. If the court supervises your Will then any deviation from the instructions given in your Will can be made only for good cause and with court approval.

# YOUR WILL — YOUR WAY

Many people decide that the Will is the best route to go but do not act upon it, thinking it unnecessary to prepare a Will until they are very old and about to die. But according to reports published by the National Center for Health Statistics (a division of the U.S. Department of Health and Human Services) 2 of every 10 people who die in any given year are under the age of 60. Twenty percent may seem like a small number until it hits close to home as it did with a young couple. The couple was having difficulty conceiving a child. They went from doctor to doctor until they met someone just beginning his practice. With his knowledge of the latest advances in medicine, he was able to help them. The birth of their child was a moment of joy and gratitude. They asked a nurse to take a picture of them all together — the happy couple, the newborn child and the doctor who made it all happen. Happiness radiated from the picture, but one of them would be dead within six months.

You might think it was the child. An infant's life is so fragile. SIDS and all manner of childhood diseases can threaten a little one.
But no, he grew up to be a healthy young man.

If you looked at the picture, you might guess the husband. Overweight and stressed out; his ruddy complexion suggested high blood pressure. He looked like a typical heart- attack-prone type A personality.
No, he was fine and went on to enjoy raising his son.

Probably the wife. She had such a difficult time with the pregnancy and the delivery was especially hard. Perhaps it was all too much for her.
No, she recovered and later had two more children.

It was the doctor who was killed in a three car collision.

Though we all agree, that one never knows, still people put off making a Will figuring that if they die before getting around to it, Illinois law will take over and their property will be distributed in the manner that they would have wanted anyway. The problem with that logic is the complexity of the Rules of Descent and Distribution. If you are survived by a spouse, child, parent or sibling, then it isn't too difficult to figure out who will inherit your property. But if none of these survive you, the ultimate beneficiary of your property may not be the person you would have chosen, had you taken the time to do so.

You may think there is no rush to make a Will because you have arranged you finances so that your property will go to whom you wish, automatically, and without the need for probate. But consider that if you die as a result of an accident, someone will need to be appointed as your Representative to sue on behalf of your estate. It is better to leave a Will so that you can say who will be in charge of handling your affairs once you die. If you don't have a Will and a probate procedure is necessary then the Probate court will choose someone for you (see Page 27).

Still another benefit to making a Will is that you can make provision for who will get your personal property, including your car. Without a Will, your Representative gets to make these decisions. With a Will you can make special provision for the care of your child or grandchild. You can even provide for the care of your pet as these next few pages will show.

# MAKE A GIFT OF YOUR CAR

As explained in Chapter 6, if you are married at the time of your death, then your spouse can transfer that car to his/her name. All your spouse need do is to take the title to the car and a certified copy of the death certificate to the local Drivers License facility.

If you do not have a surviving spouse or surviving child, then consider making a gift of your car in your Will. If you do so, then it will be relatively simple for your car to be transferred to the beneficiary. If you do not make a specific gift of your car in your Will, then it becomes part of your probate estate. Your Representative can sell the car and include the proceeds of the sale in the estate funds to be distributed to your residuary beneficiaries. If all of the residuary beneficiaries agree, the Representative can give the car to one of them as part of that beneficiary's share of the estate. If you die intestate, the car will go to your next of kin.

## JOINT OWNERSHIP
Some may think it just as easy to hold the car jointly with the intended beneficiary, because once one owner dies, the other owns the car without any need for probate — but the problem with joint ownership of a motor vehicle is liability. If either owner is in an accident with the car, then both may be liable for any damage that is done. If you are single, the better route is to hold title to the car in your name only and make a gift of the car in your Will.

# FOR PET LOVERS

A woman died at peace,
leaving her fortune
and care of her cat to her niece.
Alas, the fortune and the cat
Soon disappeared after that.

You could make provision in your Will for the care of your pet, but the moral of the above limerick, is that leaving your money to someone to do the job may not be the best route to go.

 ## TRUST FOR CARE OF PET

If you are serious about caring for your pet after your death, you can employ an attorney to set up a separate trust for the care of your pet, or you can have the attorney include a trust provision in your Will.

The trust document will direct the trustee to pay sufficient monies to a custodian for the care of the pet. You also need to name a beneficiary (a person or charitable organization) to receive whatever may remain in the trust after the pet dies.

If you intend the trustee to also serve as custodian of the pet, then you can ask the beneficiary to regularly check on the pet to see to it that the pet is treated humanely, if not benevolently.

## CARE OF PETS (Continued)

If you don't have the resources to set up a trust to care for your pet, you can still ask a fellow pet lover to care for the animal. If no one among your circle of family and friends is able to do so, then ask your pet's veterinarian to consider starting an "Orphaned Pet Service" to assist in finding new homes for pets who lose their owners. It is good public relations and a potential source of income. People can make provision in their Will to pay the Veterinarian to care for the pet until a suitable family can be found. That is a more humane approach than the, all too common practice, of putting a pet "to sleep" rather than have the pet suffer the loss of its master. And in at least one case, that reasoning backfired.

Eleanor always had a pet in the house. After her husband died, her two poodles were her constant companions. When Eleanor became ill with cancer, she worried about what would happen to her "buddies" if she died. She finally decided it best to have her family put them to sleep when she died.

Eleanor endured surgery, chemotherapy, radiation therapy, and even some holistic remedies, but she continued to go downhill. Eleanor's family came in to visit her at the hospital to say their last good-byes. She was so ill, she didn't even recognize them. No one thought she could last the day. Because the family was from out of state, and time short, they decided to put the pets to sleep so they need only take care of the funeral arrangements when she died. To everyone's surprise, Eleanor rallied. She lived two more long, lonely years. She often said she wished they had put her to sleep instead of her buddies.

# FOR PARENTS OF A MINOR CHILD

Parents have a special responsibility. They need to make provision for the care of their child in the event they both die or become incapacitated before the child is grown. It is unusual for a child to lose both parents, but it does happen, and parents need to provide for this possibility.

## CARING FOR THE PERSON OF THE CHILD

A child must be cared for in two ways, the *person* of the child and *property* of the child. To care for the person of the child, someone must be in charge of the child's everyday living, not only food and shelter but to provide social, ethical and religious training. Someone must have legal authority to make medical decisions and see to the child's education.

To care for the property of the child, someone must take charge of monies left to the child. That person is responsible to see that the monies are used for the care of the child and that anything left over is preserved until the child becomes an adult.

Illinois Statute (755 ILCS 5/11-5.3) gives parents the right to appoint a STANDBY GUARDIAN to care for the person and property of their minor child in the event that they both are unable to do so. They can make this appointment by signing a DESIGNATION OF STANDBY GUARDIAN. Both parents must sign the Designation so that there is no conflict in their choice of guardian. The statutory form of the Designation can be found in any law library or you can download it from the internet:

http://www.legis.state.il.us/

The person named as Standby Guardian can assume the care of the child upon the death or incapacity of the last surviving parent, but that person needs to ask the Probate court to be appointed as the child's legal guardian. In appointing a guardian, the judge's primary concern is the best interests of the child. The judge will give priority to the person you chose as Standby Guardian, but if the judge determines that person is not qualified to be the child's guardian, he will appoint someone who is (755 ILCS 5/11-5.3 (b)).

## LEAVING PROPERTY FOR THE CHILD

As any parent is well aware, it is expensive to raise a child. People that you might consider to be the best choice to serve as your child's guardian might not be able to do so unless you leave sufficient monies to pay for the care of the child. If you are a person of limited finances, then consider purchasing a term life insurance policy on your life and/or on the life of the other parent of the child. If you can only afford one policy, then insure the life of the parent who contributes most to the support of the child.

Term insurance policies are relatively inexpensive if you limit the term to just that period of time until your child becomes an adult. Some companies offer a combination of term life and disability insurance. As with any other purchase, it is important to comparison shop to obtain the best price for the coverage.

# FOR PARENTS OF A MINOR CHILD (continued)

If you are married to the parent of your child, then the beneficiary of the term insurance policy can be your spouse with your child as an alternate beneficiary. Married or single, you can name your child as the primary beneficiary of the policy.

If you name the child as beneficiary of the policy that is no more than $10,000 in value, and you die before the child turns 18, then a guardian of the property, will need to be appointed to take custody of the insurance proceeds. In such case, the judge usually appoints the surviving parent as the guardian. The court will not allow the court appointed guardian of the property, to spend any of the insurance funds without court approval. The court will require that the guardian give the court an annual accounting to be sure that the monies are being preserved for the benefit of the child. Once the child turns 18, the court will supervise the distribution of the monies to the child (755 ILCS 5/25-20, 5/11-7, 5/11-13).

If the other parent is able to care for the child, then it is best to avoid guardianship proceedings because they can be both time-consuming and expensive. If you are planning to leave a significant amount of insurance funds to your child then the better route might be to name a custodian for the insurance funds under the UNIFORM TRANSFERS TO MINORS ACT (see page 169) or perhaps consult with an attorney about setting up a trust for the child as explained on the next page.

## ☎ LAWYER | PREPARE A TRUST FOR THE CHILD

If you have sufficient monies to care for your child until adulthood, then consult with an attorney about setting up a trust for the child or drafting a Will with a trust provision in the event you die before the child is grown. You will need to appoint a trustee to handle the trust funds as the child is growing. You can appoint the other parent of the child as the trustee. You will need to appoint a successor trustee in the event that the other parent is unable to serve as trustee.

You can appoint the same person to serve as trustee as you have chosen to serve as Standby Guardian, but it may be better to appoint two different people for these jobs. The desirable qualities of a guardian are essentially that of a "people person" someone who is sensitive to the child's emotional needs — someone who will love and nurture the child.

The qualities of importance in a trustee are honesty, trustworthiness and being knowledgeable in money matters. The trustee will be in charge of giving sufficient money to the guardian for the child's maintenance. Consider choosing a trustee who is not overly generous so that all of the funds will be spent before the child is grown, yet not so thrifty that the child has little quality of life in his formative years.

If you are successful in your choice, the child will be fortunate to have two such adults to guide him through his childhood.

# PROVIDING FOR THE STEPCHILD

Perhaps the reason that the story of Cinderella has such universal appeal, is that many stepchildren, at one point or another, feel left out. Even the law seems to reinforce that perception. For example, if you have a stepchild, then that child has no intestate rights to your estate unless you happen to die intestate with absolutely no surviving relations, in which case the child of your last deceased spouse can inherit your property (see page 107). If you and your spouse hold all property jointly, and your spouse dies first, then your stepchild will be left nothing unless you make some provision for the child in your Will.

Should your spouse die, then you, and not your stepchild, have the authority to agree to an autopsy or an anatomical gift. Even during your spouse's lifetime, you, and not your stepchild, have the authority to make your spouse's medical decisions in the event that your spouse becomes incapacitated.

Of course, giving you authority to make your spouse's medical decisions and giving you the right to inherit all of your spouse's estate must be a decision that is agreeable to your spouse. If your spouse wants the child to have primary authority to make medical decisions, then your spouse can sign a Power of Attorney For Health Care and appoint the child (and not you) as Health Care Agent (see page 161). Similarly, if your spouse wants his/her child to inherit property, then your spouse can arrange his/her finances so that the child will inherit the property. Hopefully, your spouse will consult with an estate planning attorney who can explain the best way to achieve that goal, else that intent could be thwarted and the child end up with nothing, as was the case in the example given on page 117.

# PROVIDING FOR THE ADULT CHILD

It isn't just stepchildren who can be left out if no provision is made. Even children from a long-standing marriage can be cut off against the wishes of a parent. A parent may assume that all of their children will be treated equally once they are both gone, but consider that the last to die is the one who gets to decide "who gets what." That was the case with Joan and Herbert. They were a devoted couple, married over forty years. Herb was the breadwinner, but he was content to let Joan handle all of the finances.

Joan wanted to be sure that each of their three daughters would always have a decent place to live. They purchased a three story house and each of the daughters moved into a different floor of the home. It was the parent's intent that once they were both gone, the daughters would inherit and occupy the building.

The couple held everything jointly. When Joan died, all of their property, including the home, was owned by Herbert. The grief suffered by Herbert at his wife's passing was more than he could bear. He alternated between sadness, despair and anger.

His middle daughter took the brunt of his anger. Their relationship had always been strained. She felt she could never live up to her father's expectations. She was not the cute baby of the family as was her younger sister. She was not the eldest daughter who always seemed to make her Dad proud. He always made her feel that she was a disappointment to him. Once her mother died, she had no one left to buffer the relationship with her father.

Within three months of Joan's death, Herbert had an attorney draft a Will leaving all to his eldest and youngest daughter. None of the children knew what he had done.

Herbert decided to take a trip to Europe to try to escape the pain of his mourning. When he was in France, he suffered a massive heart attack and died. It was less than 6 months from the time of Joan's death.

Had he returned from Europe, he may have reconciled with his daughter, but as it happened, there was no time for them to develop a better relationship.

With both their parents gone, the eldest and youngest daughter decided to sell the home. The youngest sister offered some of the proceeds to middle daughter. The middle daughter refused the offer with unkind words. Being offered less than her one-third share, meant to her that her sisters approved of their father's action. It was as if she were being disinherited all over again.

It was unfortunate that Joan's best plans were thwarted. They didn't have to be. She and Herbert could have kept a life estate in the property with the remainder going to all three girls. That would have ensured that each daughter received an equal inheritance. More importantly, the family would not have been torn by the hurt and anger that was more a product of a husband's grief rather than the absence of a father's love.

 **LAWYER**

## A SPECIAL NEEDS TRUST FOR THE INCAPACITATED

If a person is incapacitated, both the federal and state government provide assistance with programs such as social security disability benefits and custodial nursing home care under the Medicaid program. The family often supplements the government estate program by providing for the incapacitated person's *special needs*, such as clothing, hobbies, special education, outings to a movie or special event — things that give the incapacitated person some quality of life.

To be eligible for government assistance programs the incapacitated must be essentially without funds. Caretakers fear that leaving money to the incapacitated in a will or trust will disqualify the incapacitated from further government assistance. Understanding this dilemma, the federal government allows caretakers to set up a *Special Needs* trust with the incapacitated as the beneficiary of the trust. One type of Special Needs Trust is the *Disability Trust* as authorized by 42 U.S.C. 1382c(a)(3). This trust may be established by a caretaker for an incapacitated person who is under the age of 65. A trustee is appointed to use trust funds to provide for the special needs of the incapacitated. If any trust funds are left after the incapacitated dies, then those funds must be used to reimburse the state for monies spent on behalf of the incapacitated person.

There are other types of special needs trusts that are allowed under the law. An experienced Elder Law an attorney can explain the different options available and assist the family member in preparing a Will or trust that will provide for the incapacitated person's special needs once the family member dies.

 **LAWYER**

# PROVIDING FOR
# THE INCAPACITATED

If you are the caretaker or legal guardian of someone who is incapacitated, then in addition to preparing your own estate plan, you need to be concerned about what will happen to the incapacitated person should you die. Someone will need to make medical decisions for the incapacitated person and see to it that he/she is properly housed and fed.

### APPOINTMENT OF A SUCCESSOR CARETAKER

Often a family member will agree to take responsibility for the care of an incapacitated person in the event that the caretaker dies. But perhaps no one wants the job, or the opposite case, too many want to have control. For example, if a parent is incapacitated, one child may want the parent to remain at home with the assistance of a home health care worker. Another child may think the best place for the parent is an assisted living facility with 24 hour care. The caretaker spouse may be concerned that a tug-of-war will erupt once he dies.

In such case, the caretaker should consult with an attorney to ensure future care for the incapacitated person. The attorney may suggest establishing a trust or having a legal guardian appointed for the incapacitated person while the parent/caretaker is alive. Once the guardianship is in place, the court will continue to supervise the care of the incapacitated person until he/she dies.

# PROVIDING FOR YOUR OWN INCAPACITY

As the life expectancy of the population increases, so does the percentage of the population who suffer from debilitating diseases such Alzheimer's and Parkinsons'. As you age, your chances for suffering dementia as a result of a stroke or other debilitating diseases increases. It is estimated that more than 50% of the population who are 85 or older, suffer from some degree of dementia.

If you are concerned that you may become disabled in the future, you need to consider who will care for your property and who will take care of your person. You can have an attorney prepare a trust. You can be trustee of the funds while you have capacity. Once you can no longer do so, then the person you name as Successor Trustee will take over. Your attorney can also draft a document naming someone to serve as the guardian of your person. In the event that it is necessary to appoint someone to be your guardian, then that person will be given priority (755 ILCS 5/11a-6).

If you do not have sufficient assets to justify the cost of employing an attorney to draft these documents, you can appoint someone to make your medical decisions by signing a Power of Attorney for Health Care (see page 160). You can also appoint someone to be your Agent to care for your property in the event you become incapacitated by signing a Power of Attorney For Property. Your attorney can prepare both of these documents to meet your special needs or you can use the statutory form provided by the state of Illinois, namely (755 ILCS 45/4-10) for the Power of Attorney for Health Care and (755 ILCS 45/3-3) for the Power of Attorney For Property. You can find these statutes at most Public Libraries or you can download them from the Internet (http://www.legis.state.il.us/).

# ARRANGING TO PAY BILLS

When people draft a Will they are more concerned about giving their possessions away than they are about taking into account what they actually have to give.    This was the case with Larry.    He had no family to speak of.  After his wife died, he bought a condominium in Springfield. Over the years, he developed a close network of friends. They became his family.  Larry did not have much money. His car was leased.  He had a mortgage on the condominium.  He wanted his friends to know how much they meant to him so he had a Will drafted giving all he owned to five close friends.

The friends appreciated the gesture but the probate procedure turned out to be a nightmare.  They had to keep current the mortgage payments and the maintenance fees until the condominium was sold.   Because Larry left little cash, this money had to come out of the beneficiaries' pockets. Two were living on their social security income and they had to borrow money from the others to contribute to their share of the upkeep.

The beneficiaries had no money to settle the lease on the car.   Even if they did, they decided that there was no point in doing so because the amount needed to obtain clear title was greater than the current market value of the car.   The beneficiaries decided not to make any further payment and they returned  the car to the leasing agent.  Their decision turned out to be a losing proposition. The leasing agent took the car, sold it and then sued the estate for the balance of the monies owed on the lease.

Because the beneficiaries had to quickly liquidate the estate, the condominium sold for less than it would have had they the time, energy and resources to fix it up. After they settled with the leasing agent, paid off the funeral expenses, mortgage, and probate fees there was only a few hundred dollars left. That was a lot of work and stress for nothing.

The pity was that Larry could have arranged his finances so that his beneficiaries were not burdened by his debt. He could have taken out mortgage insurance as part of the loan package. In most cases the cost of the insurance is nominal and is included as part of the monthly mortgage payment.

Larry could have done the same when he leased the car. Most leasing contracts offer term life insurance as an option. The cost of such insurance depends on the age of the person, the term of the loan and the amount of monies owed, but the premium paid each month is just a small fraction of the loan payment.

Even if Larry just arranged for payment of one of these debts, his beneficiaries would have come away with the gift that Larry intended, instead of the headache that they inherited.

# PROVIDE FOR CREDIT CARD DEBT

If you have significant credit card debt, you need to consider how that debt will be paid once you die. Most credit card companies offer insurance policies and include the premium as part of your monthly payment. If you have such insurance, then should you die, any outstanding balance is paid. It benefits the credit card company to offer life insurance as part of the credit package, because they are assured of prompt payment should the borrower die. However, if you have little or no assets and no one other than yourself is liable to pay the debt, you may have no incentive to pay for insurance that can only benefit the lender.

As discussed in Chapters 2 and 4, if you hold a credit card jointly with another person, both of you are equally liable to pay the debt. If one of you dies, the other is responsible to pay the bill regardless of who ran up the bill. If paying that bill could be a struggle for the surviving debtor, then the better route to go is for each of you to have your own credit card.

Still another reason not to hold a joint credit card is that each of you can establish your own line of credit. This is especially important if you are married and one of you is retired or has been out of the job market for any period of time. Should the breadwinner die, it may be difficult for the surviving partner to establish credit if he/she has no recent work record It is easier for the unemployed spouse to establish a line of credit when he/she is married to someone who is working.

# PURCHASE LIFE INSURANCE

The good part of purchasing loan insurance — be it credit card insurance, mortgage insurance or car insurance, is that you can usually purchase the insurance without taking a medical examination. The down side, is that such insurance may be more expensive than a life insurance policy. If you are in fairly good health, consider taking out a life insurance policy to cover all of your outstanding loans. The cost of the single life insurance policy may be significantly less than purchasing separate loan insurance policies.

The estate planning strategy of purchasing life insurance to pay off all of your loans works best if you are married and your spouse is jointly liable for your debts. If you name your spouse as beneficiary of the life insurance policy, then he/she can use the life insurance funds to pay off all monies owed. If you name someone as beneficiary who has no legal obligation to pay your debts and if your primary residence is in the State of Illinois, none of your creditors can force your beneficiary to use any part of those funds to pay your debts (735 ILCS 5/12-1001 f). If you want the insurance funds used to pay your debts, then this may not be the way to go. But, if you want to be sure that someone receives money for their care after you are gone, and you do not want those funds reduced by the cost of probate or to pay off your debts, then this strategy should accomplish your goal.

Which brings us to the issue of life insurance — should you have it? How much is enough? The answer to these questions depends on the "sleep at night" factor, namely how much insurance do you need to make you not worry about insurance coverage when you go to sleep at night? It is often more an emotional than a financial issue.

Some people have an "every man for himself" attitude and are content to have no life insurance at all. Others worry about how their loved ones will manage if they are not around to support them. The same person may have different thoughts about insurance coverage as the circumstances of their life changes — from no coverage in their bachelor days to more-than-enough coverage in their child rearing days to just-enough-to-bury-me in their senior years. Insurance companies recognize that people's needs change over the years. Many companies offer flexible insurance coverage. As with any consumer item, it is a good idea to shop around.

In addition to life insurance, you might want to consider long-term health care insurance. Your best estate plan could be sabotaged by a lengthy, or debilitating illness. If you are poor, long-term nursing care may not be of concern to you, because all your needs should be covered under Medicaid. If you are very wealthy, you may not worry because you have more than enough money to pay for your care. But the rest of us need to think about ways to provide for long-term health care. An experienced Elder law attorney can suggest an estate plan that will preserve your assets in the event of a lengthy illness.

If long-term care insurance is part of your estate plan, then you need to consider the many plans that are available. You can get shopper's guides to long-term care insurance, free of charge, from the Illinois Department of Aging (800) 548-9034. They are also available to answer specific questions that you may have. The Illinois Department of Insurance has long-term care insurance information available at their Web site:

 ILLINOIS DEPARTMENT OF INSURANCE
http://www.state.il.us/ins/

# ANNUITIES TO SPREAD THE INHERITANCE

Most beneficiaries go through their inheritance within two years. For many, the reason the money is gone so soon, is that there just wasn't much money to inherit in the first place. But for others, it's a spending frenzy.

People's spending habits remain much the same throughout their lifetime. Some people are squirrels, always saving for the winter. For others, it's:

Earn-A-Penny    Spend-A-Penny

Most of us fall somewhere in between. We are not extravagant in our spending habits, yet it is a struggle to save. But why should we struggle to purchase an insurance policy if the intended beneficiary will spend it in a few months?

If you want to leave an insurance policy benefit to someone you love, but the intended beneficiary is immature, or a born spendthrift, then a simple solution to the problem may be to purchase an annuity rather than life insurance. The annuity can be set up so that the beneficiary receives money on a monthly, or yearly basis, rather than a single lump sum payment when you die. There are many different types of annuities, so again, it is important to shop around.

# CHOOSING THE RIGHT ESTATE PLAN

*Joint Ownership?*
*A POD Account?*
*A TOD Account?*
*A Trust?*
*A Will?*
*An Insurance Policy???*

This chapter offers so many options that the reader may be more confused than when he was blissfully unenlightened.

As with most things in life, you may find there are no ultimate solutions, just alternatives. The right choice for you is the one that best accomplishes your goal. This being the case, you first need to determine what you want to accomplish with the money that you leave. Think about what will happen to your property if you were to die suddenly, without making any plan different from the one you now have.
Who will get your property?
Will there be any estate tax?
Will they need to go through a full probate procedure?

If the answers to these questions are not what you wish, then you need to work to retitle your property to accomplish your goals. For those with significant assets, — especially those with estates large enough to pay estate taxes, a trip to an experienced Estate Planning attorney may be well worth the consultation fee.

Once you are satisfied with your estate plan, then the final thing to determine is whether your heirs will be able to locate your assets once you are deceased.

Most people have their business records in one place, their Will in another place, car titles and deeds in still another place. When someone dies, their beneficiaries may feel as if they are playing a game of "hide and seek" with the decedent. The game might be fun if it were not for the fact that things not found may be forever lost. For example, suppose you die in an accident and no one knows you are insured by your credit card company for accidental death in the amount of $25,000. The only one to profit is the insurance company, which is just that much richer because no one told them that you died as a result of an accident.

How about a key to a safe deposit box located in another state? Will anyone find it? Even if they find the key, how will they find the box?

It is not difficult to arrange things so that your affairs are always in order. It amounts to being aware of what you own (and owe) and keeping a record of your possessions. A side benefit is that by doing so, you will always know where all your business records are. If you ever spent time trying to collect information to file your taxes or trying to find a lost stock or bond certificate, you will appreciate the value of organizing your records.

Heirs need all the help they can get. It is difficult enough dealing with the loss, none the less trying to locate important documents. Your heirs will have no problem locating your assets if you keep all of your records a single place. It can be a desk drawer or a file cabinet or even a shoe box. If you wish to keep all of your original documents in a safe deposit box, then make a copy of each document and keep the copy in your home with a note saying where the original can be found. It is helpful if you keep a separate file or folder for each type of investment. You might consider setting up the following folders:

---

📁 **THE BANK & SECURITIES FOLDER**

The BANK & SECURITIES FOLDER is for original certificates of deposit, stock, bonds or mutual funds. The folder should contain a copy of the contract you signed with each financial institution. The contract will show where you have funds and who you named as beneficiary or joint owner of the account. If someone owes you money and has signed a Promissory note or mortgage that identifies you as the lender, then you can store such documents in this folder as well.

If you have a safe deposit box, then keep a record of the location of the box and box number in this folder. Make a copy of all of the items in the box (including jewelry), and place the copies in a folder entitled CONTENTS OF SAFE DEPOSIT BOX. You may wish to attach an envelope to the folder and put your safe deposit key in that envelope. As explained on page 70, it may take a court order to remove items from the box once you die. Consider allowing someone you trust to be able to gain entry to the box in the event of your incapacity or death.

---

## 📁  THE DEED FOLDER

Many people save every scrap of paper associated with the closing of real property.   If you closed recently on real estate and there was a mortgage involved in the purchase, you probably walked away from closing with enough paper to wallpaper your kitchen. If you wish, you can keep all of those papers in a separate file that identifies the property, for example:

CLOSING PAPERS FOR THE METROPOLIS PROPERTY.

Set aside the original deed (or a copy if the original is in a safe deposit box) and place it into a separate DEED FOLDER. Include deeds to parcels of real  property, cemetery deeds, condominium deeds, cooperative shares to real property, timesharing certificates,  etc. Include deeds to out of  state  property as well as Illinois property in the DEED FOLDER.  If you have a mortgage on your property, then put a copy of the mortgage and promissory note in a separate LIABILITY FOLDER.

## 📁  THE INSURANCE/PENSION FOLDER

The INSURANCE  FOLDER is for each original insurance policy that you own, be it car insurance, homeowner's insurance or a health care insurance policy.  If you purchased real property, you probably received a title commitment at closing and the original title insurance policy some weeks later when you received your original deed from recording.  If you cannot locate the title insurance policy, then contact the closing agent and have them send you a copy of your title policy.  If you have a pension or an annuity, then include those documents in this folder as well.

#  THE PERSONAL PROPERTY FOLDER

### MOTOR VEHICLES

Put all motor vehicle titles in Personal Property folder. This includes cars, mobile homes, boats, planes, etc. If you owe money on the vehicle, the lender may have possession of the title certificate. If such is the case, then put a copy of the registration in this folder and a copy of the promissory note or chattel mortgage in a separate liability folder.

If you have a boat or plane, then identify the location of the motor vehicle. For example, if you are leasing space in an airplane hanger or in a marina, then keep a copy of the leasing agreement in this file.

### JEWELRY

If you own expensive jewelry, then keep a picture of the item together with the sales receipt or written appraisal in this folder.

### COLLECTOR'S ITEMS

If you own a valuable art collection, or a coin collection or any other item of significant value, then include a picture of the item in this file. Also include evidence of ownership of the item, such as a sales receipt or a certificate of authenticity, or a written appraisal of the property.

*When Someone Dies In Illinois*

## 📁 THE LIABILITY FOLDER

The LIABILITY FOLDER should contain all loan documents of debts that you owe. For example, if you purchased real property and have a mortgage on that property, then put a copy of the mortgage and promissory note in this folder. If you owe money on a car, then put the promissory note and chattel mortgage on the car in the file. If you have a credit card, then put a copy of the contract you signed with the credit card company in this file.

Many people never take the time to calculate their *net worth* (what a person owns less what that person owes). By having a record of your outstanding debts, you can calculate your net worth whenever you wish.

## 📁 THE TAX RECORD FOLDER

Your Personal Representative (or next of kin) will need to file your final income tax return. Keep a copy of your tax returns (both federal and state) for the past three years in your Tax Record Folder.

# 🗁 THE PERSONAL RECORD FOLDER

The PERSONAL RECORD FOLDER should include documents that relate to you personally, such as a birth certificate, naturalization papers, pre-nuptial or post- nuptial agreement, Will or Trust, marriage certificate, divorce papers, army records, social security card; etc. If you have a Health Care Directive or a Power of Attorney, then this is a good place to keep those documents.

## FOR FEDERAL RETIREES

If you are a Federal Retiree, then you should have received your **PERSONAL IDENTIFICATION NUMBER (PIN)** and the person who will inherit your pension (your *survivor annuitant*) should have received his/her own PIN as well. It is relatively simple to obtain this during your lifetime, but it may be difficult and/or stressful for your survivor annuitant to work through the system once you are gone. To get information on obtaining these numbers you can call the RETIREMENT INFORMATION OFFICE at (888) 767-6738. For the hearing impaired, call (800) 878-5707.

Upon your death, your survivor annuitant may be entitled to death benefits. These benefits are not automatic. Your survivor annuitant must apply for them by submitting a death claim to the Office of Personnel Management. Your survivor needs to know that it is necessary to apply and also how to apply. See page 30 for an explanation about how to apply for benefits and then make that information available to your family. You can either put this information in the insurance/pension folder or in your Personal Record folder.

# THE *If I Die* FILE

In addition to keeping your up-to-date records in a single place, you need to let your family know the location of these items. You can set up an *If I Die* file and give that file to your next of kin or the person you appointed as Personal Representative in your Will.

You can use the form on the next page as a basis for the information to include in the file.

# *If I Die*

then the following information will help settle my estate:

## INFORMATION FOR DEATH CERTIFICATE

MY FULL LEGAL NAME _____

MY SOCIAL SECURITY NO. _____

MY USUAL OCCUPATION _____

BIRTH DATE AND BIRTH PLACE _____

If naturalized, date & place _____

MY FATHER'S NAME _____

MY MOTHER'S MAIDEN NAME _____

## PERSONS TO BE NOTIFIED OF MY DEATH

_____

_____

_____

## FUNERAL AND BURIAL ARRANGEMENTS

LOCATION OF BURIAL SITE

_____

LOCATION OF PRENEED FUNERAL CONTRACT

_____

---

FOR VETERAN or SPOUSE BURIAL IN A NATIONAL CEMETERY

BRANCH_____SERIAL NO._____

VETERAN'S RANK _____

VETERAN'S VA CLAIM NUMBER _____

DATE AND PLACE OF ENTRY INTO SERVICE:

_____

DATE AND PLACE OF SEPARATION FROM SERVICE:

_____

LOCATION OF OFFICIAL MILITARY DISCHARGE
OR DD 214 FORM_____

---

# LOCATION OF LEGAL DOCUMENTS

BIRTH CERTIFICATE _____

MARRIAGE CERTIFICATE_____

DIVORCE DECREE _____

PASSPORT _____

WILL OR TRUST _____

DEEDS _____

MORTGAGES _____

TITLE TO MOTOR VEHICLES _____

HEALTH CARE DIRECTIVES _____

NAME, PHONE NO. OF ATTORNEY_____

# LOCATION OF FINANCIAL RECORDS

INSURANCE POLICIES:

NAME OF COMPANY & PHONE NO. _____

LOCATION OF POLICY _____

BENEFICIARY OF POLICY _____

PENSIONS/ANNUITIES:

IF FEDERAL RETIREE: PIN NUMBER: _____

NAME OF SURVIVOR _____

SURVIVOR PIN NUMBER _____

BANK

BANK: ACCOUNT NO._____

NAME, ADDRESS OF FINANCIAL INSTITUTION

_____

LOCATION OF SAFE DEPOSIT BOX _____

LOCATION OF KEY TO BOX _____

SECURITIES

NAME AND PHONE NUMBER OF BROKER

_____

TAX RECORDS FOR PAST 3 YEARS

LOCATION _____

ACCOUNTANT: NAME, PHONE # _____

_____

# WHEN TO UPDATE YOUR ESTATE PLAN

We discussed people's natural disinclination to make an estate plan until they are faced with their own mortality. Many believe that they will make just one Will and then die (maybe that's why they put off making a Will). The reality is, that most people who make a Will change it at least once before they die.

If you have an estate plan, it is important to update it when any of the following things take place:

## ✍ RELOCATION TO A NEW STATE OR COUNTRY

If you move within state then there is no need to change your estate plan, but if you move to another state or country, then you need to check to see whether your plan is valid in that state. Each state (and country) has its own laws relating to the inheritance of property and those laws are very different from each other. Items that are protected from a creditor in one state, may not be creditor proof in another state. Each state has its own estate tax structure. If estate taxes are high, you may need an estate plan that will minimize the impact of those taxes.

Each state has its own, unique, laws of intestate succession. Who has the right to inherit your property in one state may be very different from who can inherit your property in another. The rights of a spouse in a community property state are really different from those in other states. Even if you have a Will, what one state considers to be a valid Will, may be very different from what another state considers to be valid. If you move to another state or country, then it is important to either educate yourself about the laws of the state, or to consult with an attorney who can assist you in reviewing your estate plan to see if that plan will accomplish your goals in that state.

## ✍ A SIGNIFICANT CHANGE IN THE LAW

It is important to keep up with changes in the law. You can do so by just reading your daily newspaper. Happily, laws relating to the inheritance of property and the way estates are probated, have remained  stable over the years. Tax laws however, are in a constant state of flux. You need to be aware of how the tax structure is being changed and how that change affects your estate plan.

## ✍ A CHANGE IN RELATIONSHIP

If you get married, divorced, have a child, lose a beneficiary of your estate, then you should examine your estate plan to determine whether it needs to be revised. If your marriage is annulled or you get divorced, there are certain changes that take place by law. For example, unless the final judgment of dissolution says differently, homestead owned as husband and wife becomes property owned as  tenants-in-common and not with any rights of survivorship. But it is important to not just rely on the law because the law may change or have exceptions that are unknown to you. For example, current law provides that if you divorce and afterward decide to live together in other property as  your homestead, then each spouse has rights of survivorship in that property (765 ILCS 1005/1c). Best to change all documents after the divorce. That includes deeds, Wills, Powers of Attorney, beneficiaries of insurance policies, pension plans, etc.

# GAMES DECEDENTS PLAY

We discussed the game of "hide and seek" some decedents play with their heirs. A variation of that game is the "wild goose chase." The decedent never updates his files, so his records are filled with all sorts of lapsed insurance policies, promissory notes of debts long since paid; brokerage statements of securities that have been sold. The family wastes time trying to locate the "missing" asset.

The best joke is to keep the key to a safe deposit box that you are no longer leasing. That will keep folks hunting for a long time!

If you do not have a wicked sense of humor, then do your family a favor and update your records on a regular basis.

# Completing The Process  9

The funeral is over.

Everyone went home.

You experienced and got past the initial grief.

All the affairs of the decedent have been settled.

You even did some of the things suggested in Chapters 7 and 8 so you feel that your own affairs are now in order. But is the grieving over? Do you have closure? To use a tired expression, have you been able to "get on with your life" or do you find that you are still grieving?

And how about the children in the decedent's life? How are they taking the loss?

The death event is not over until the family finally finds peace and acceptance of the loss. This chapter deals with issues that may arise as the family goes through the grieving process.

# THE GRIEVING PROCESS

Psychologists have observed that it is common for a person to go through a series of stages as part of the grieving process.    There is the initial shock of the death and often disbelief and denial:

"He can't be dead.   I just spoke to him today!"

It is common for a mourner to be angry — angry at the decedent for dying — angry at a family member for something he should or shouldn't have done — just plain angry.

Sometimes an ill person is aware of his  impending death and becomes angry, as  if mourning his own death. Relations with the family may become strained  under the stress of the illness.   If there was an argument with the decedent, the bereaved may be left with an unresolved conflict and feelings of guilt.

Mourners often experience guilt. Many have an uneasy feeling that the death was somehow their fault. Some regret not having spent more time with the decedent. Others  feel guilty because they weren't present when the decedent died.

There is grieving even when death is long expected and even welcomed. This was the case with a wife who nursed her husband at  home for nine long years. Her  husband suffered from debilitating strokes, a chronic heart condition, and  finally failing  kidneys. She often said "Some things are worse than death."  When he died, she was  surprised at the depth of her emotions.

Although professionals in the fields of psychiatry and psychology have observed that guilt and anger are stages of grieving, there is no agreement about the number or composition of the stages of grieving. This is not surprising. The ways people react to death is as diverse as there are people. Some people seem not to grieve at all. Whether such people experience any stage of the grieving process may not be known even to the person himself/herself.

And there is diversity in grieving even in the same person. Each circumstance of death in one's life is different from another, so a person will grieve differently when different people in their life die. But for purposes of this discussion, we note that many people who lose someone they love report experiencing the following emotions and in the following sequence:

> initial shock, disbelief, alarm
> numbness, anger, guilt
> pining, searching for the deceased
> sadness, depression, loneliness
> recovery, acceptance of the loss, peace

# COPING WITH THE LOSS

How the general population deals with the death of a loved one was investigated in 1995 by the AMERICAN ASSOCIATION OF RETIRED PERSONS ("AARP"). AARP asked National Communications Research to conduct a telephone survey of over 5,000 people aged 40 or older. Approximately one third of the respondents reported that they had experienced the loss of a close friend or family member within the past year.   Those reporting a loss were asked to describe specific   coping activities that they had engaged in since the death of their loved one.

    67%  reported talking with friends and family
    16%  read an article or book about how
          to cope with death
     9%  received help with legal
          or practical arrangements
     5%  attended a grief support group

When asked what strategies they found to be most helpful in coping with their loss:

    28%  said talking with a friend or family
          member  was  most helpful
    24%  said their religion was most helpful
    10%  said knowing it was for the best
     6%  said memories of the deceased
     4%  reported staying  busy as the best strategy.

It is interesting to note that 67% of the people who suffered a loss  turned to family and friends to help them cope with the loss. Although talking with family and friends topped the list as the most commonly used strategy, only 28% reported  this as being most  helpful to them.  Many times friends and family members want to help but they are at a loss as to what to say or do.   The next section discusses different techniques that can be used to help with the grieving process.

# HELPING THE BEREAVED

Family and friends want to help the person who is grieving, but sometimes they don't know how to do it. They may feel just as helpless in dealing with the loss as does the bereaved — not knowing what to say to console those grieving.

There are no magic words, but saying you are sorry for the loss is appropriate and generally well received. Avoid platitudes such as: "It was fate." "It was God's will." "It was for the best." Especially avoid telling the bereaved that you know how he/she feels. People who suffer a great loss do not believe that anyone can understand how they feel; and they are probably correct. It is better to tell the bereaved what you are feeling:

"I was shocked when I heard of the death."
"I am so sad for you."
"I am going to really miss him."

Knowing that you share the feeling of loss is comforting to someone who is grieving.

Listening is more important than talking to the bereaved. They may need to explore the circumstances of the death — how the person died; where and when he died, etc. They may need to express what they are feeling, whether it be grief or anger. Try not to change the subject just because you are uncomfortable with the topic or with the expression of emotion.

If the bereaved wishes to reminisce about the decedent, then join in the conversation. Talk about the decedent's good qualities and the enjoyable times that you shared.

If during the funeral period, you want to do something such as prepare food or send flowers, then consider asking the bereaved for permission to do so. The family may prefer donations to a favorite charity in place of flowers. The family may have already made dinner plans for the guests. Do not make general offers of assistance. "Let me know if you need anything" is not likely to get a response even if the bereaved does need help with something. A better, more sincere, approach is a specific offer, such as, "If you need transportation, I can drive you to the cemetery."

Your assistance during the post-funeral period is more important than during the funeral period. During the funeral the bereaved is usually surrounded by family and friends and has more than ample assistance. Any offer to help at that time may not even register because the bereaved may be numb with grief — unable to comprehend what is going on around them — unable to even recall who was present at the funeral, nonetheless who offered to assist them.

Once the funeral is over and everyone has gone home, that is the time to offer support. The bereaved needs to go through a transition period and must learn to live without the presence of their loved one. In general, the more dependent the bereaved was on the decedent, the more difficult the transition. In such case, you can be most helpful if you are able to offer assistance with those tasks of daily living that the bereaved is not accustomed to performing. For example, if the decedent was the sole driver in the family, then you might help the bereaved to learn to drive or at least help find public transportation. If the decedent handled all of the family finances, you might assist the bereaved in bill paying and balancing a checkbook. If math is not your forte, help to find a bookkeeper who can assist for a reasonable fee.

But, the best thing that family and friends can do for the bereaved, is just to be there for them. As shown by the AARP survey, the specific coping activity used by the majority of the bereaved was to talk to a friend or relative. A telephone call, or a card, on a special anniversary or on a holiday will be appreciated. You can help most with a call or a visit. It is just that simple.

Also be patient with the bereaved. There is no set time to get through the grieving process. It may take considerable time for the mourner to be able to find some quality of life. If several months have passed and you are concerned that the bereaved is still not functioning well, or at least, better, then you might consider suggesting that the bereaved seek professional counseling. Try not to be judgmental when making the suggestion. Don't say "You should be feeling better by now," but rather, "I can see that you are still having a hard time getting through this difficult period. Have you considered seeing _____"

Suggest whatever is appropriate to the mourner. For example, if the mourner is a religious person, then suggest a visit with his/her religious leader. If the mourner is a social person, then suggest a support group. If the bereaved is severely depressed then a visit to a doctor or psychiatrist may be the best recommendation.

Do not expect your recommendation to be well received. The mourner may become angry or annoyed that you even made the suggestion. It may be difficult for the mourner to accept the fact that he/she needs assistance. Some people, mostly men, think it an admission of weakness to agree that they need help. They believe they should be able to "tough it out."

Some mourners may have increased their consumption of alcohol or turned to drugs in an attempt to deal with the pain that they are experiencing. If they accept your suggestion, they may need to deal with a growing addiction, in addition to the problem of overcoming the grief, and they may not be willing to do that.

Elderly people might think there is a stigma associated with any kind of counseling. They may insist "There's nothing wrong with me" fearing that you think they are unbalanced or somehow mentally defective.

Some people, especially the overachiever type, refuse to seek counseling because they perceive asking for help to be a sign of failure — an admission that they failed to work out the problem themselves. It's as if they failed "Grieving 101."

But those most resistant to a suggestion of a need for counseling are mourners who use denial as a defense mechanism. They may brush off the suggestion with "No. I'm alright" or "I'm doing a lot better." If they deny that they are having trouble getting past the grief, then they do not need to deal with the problem. If they deny that they have a problem, then they don't have the problem and that solves that!

In such cases, the timeworn adage, "You can lead a horse to water, but you can't make him drink," applies. The mourner needs to take the first step himself. You cannot take it for him. All you can do is assure the mourner (and yourself) that you have confidence that he/she can, and will, work this through.

# HELPING A CHILD THROUGH THE LOSS

The first thing parents observe about their second child is how very different that child is from their first child. Parents quickly learn that each of their children is an individual, with his/her own separate response to any given situation. It is important to keep this fact in mind when trying to assist a child through the loss of a close family member or friend. Because each child is different, there is no single proper way to assist a child through a period of mourning. You can help the child most if you consider the child's background as it relates to the loss:

What is the child's relationship to the decedent?
What were the circumstances of the death?
Was it expected or was it sudden or tragic?
What is the emotional age of the child? That age may differ significantly from his/her chronological age.

As an example, consider the family of Harold and Elaine, parents of three children. Emily, the eldest child, was one of those "born old" children, wise beyond her years, sensitive and shy. Her brother John, two years her junior was the direct opposite — boisterous, immature, constantly in motion. Peter came along five years later. He was the baby of the family, a cherub, always smiling, indulged by parents and siblings.

When their paternal grandfather died, Emily was 10, John, 8 and Peter, 3. Their parents expected the death because "Gramps" had been suffering from cancer for a long time. No mention was made to the children of the serious nature of the illness, so Emily was surprised to learn of the death. She shed no tears but retreated to her room and soon became occupied with a computer game.

John and his father cried together when they were told that Gramps had died.   Gramps was both kind and generous with a great sense of humor.   Best of all he was never critical of John's rambunctious behavior.   It seemed to John and his Dad that they lost the best friend they ever had.

Peter did not understand what was going on; but he reacted empathetically, patting John on the shoulder, and saying "Don't cry Johnny."

When it came time to go to the funeral Emily refused to go. Johnny got angry with Emily for something or another and pushed her down.   She was not hurt, but she cried loudly and carried on.   Peter started whining.   The whole day was hard on their parents.

The next few months were equally difficult.   John woke up with nightmares.   Emily was sullen and withdrawn. No one mentioned the death except Peter who was full of questions: "Where's Gramps?"
> "Was he in that box?"
> "Where did they put the box?"
> "Why was everyone crying?"

Harold and Elaine were having their own problems dealing with the loss and they had no patience with the children.   The family eventually got back to normal, but it might have been easier on all of them had the parents prepared the children for the dying process.

# PREPARING FOR THE EVENT

Most deaths are expected. The majority of people who die are ill for several months before their death. Children are not always aware of a family member's mortal illness so it comes as a shock to them when it happens. It might have been easier on Emily and John if their parents said something like:

> Gramps is old and very ill. It happens that all living
> things, plants, animals and people, eventually die.
> No one knows for sure when someone will die, but
> it may be that because he is so old and so very sick
> that Gramps may die sometime within the year.

If either child wanted to pursue the subject then that could lead to a discussion of the funeral process:

> When someone dies in our family, all of our friends
> and family gather together to talk about how much
> we loved the person and how much we will miss
> having that person with us. Later we go to the
> gravesite where we say prayers and our last good-byes.

It is important for parents to explain the children's role in this process, but like most couples, Harold and Elaine never thought about, much less discussed, their children's participation in the funeral and burial service. Had her parents told Emily what to expect and what was expected of her, she might not have objected to attending the funeral.

Before discussing the matter with the child, it is important that a husband and wife explore their own views on their children's participation in a funeral and burial. They may find that they have differing views on the following issues:

What factors should determine whether a child attends the wake and/or funeral:

- ▷ custom or convenience?
- ▷ the age and emotional maturity of that child?
- ▷ the relationship of the child to the decedent?

Should the child be allowed to decide whether he/she wishes to attend the wake and/or funeral?

Should a child be allowed (or encouraged) to touch or kiss the corpse?

Should children participate in grave site ceremonies?

Should a child be encouraged or required to visit the grave site at a later date?

There are no right or wrong answers for any of the above questions. Each family has its own set of customs and values and the answers to these questions need to conform to those customs and values. What is important is that the couple agree about what they expect of their children and then impart that expectation to their children.

The "imparting" is the difficult part. No one likes to talk about death. Parents have been told that they need to discuss sex with their children. They have been told that they need to discuss drugs with their children. These are important, life threatening, issues but it is entirely possible that a child will grow to be an adult without ever having someone close to them die. So why bring up the subject?

The reason to discuss the matter is the same reason to discuss sex with your children. The sex they see on television or hear about from their friends is a reflection of societal values but perhaps not your family values. You discuss sex to impart your family values and expectations to your children. If you wish to express to your children your views on the dying process and the afterlife (or the lack of it, if that is your belief) then it is appropriate to discuss these matters when you believe the child is sufficiently mature and ready for the discussion.

Still another reason to discuss death with the child is when someone close to them is quite aged or seriously ill. If they heard that some family member is dying, they may have concerns or questions that you can answer. Most children fear the unknown and death is an unknown to them. Of course, children are aware of the fact of death almost as soon as they can speak. It is all around them. Animated characters "die" as part of a computer game. Children's cartoon movies and television shows contain death and dying scenes. A child may have a pet that dies. Children hear about people dying almost nightly on the news.

Although children are familiar with the concept of death, they do not know how they or their family will react to the death of a loved one. If the topic is discussed prior to an impending death, the child may find it comforting to know what to expect, what behavior is expected of them, and what choices they may have regarding their attendance at a wake or funeral.

## AFTER THE FUNERAL

Once the funeral is over, you need to deal with your own loss. That may be a difficult process for you so you may not even notice that your child is also grieving. This was the case with Harold and Elaine. They were not aware that Emily was having a difficult time with the loss — after all she didn't even cry when she heard of the death. Had they thought about it, they may have realized that Emily was retreating into herself as a defense mechanism for dealing with the loss. Her continued sullen attitude after the funeral was a tip off that she was having difficulty getting beyond the loss.

If her parents had encouraged Emily to talk about the problem, they would have learned that she had ambivalent feelings about her grandfather. She loved him, but she felt that he favored her brothers. Gramps always played "boy" games of catch and touch football. He never took the time to get to know Emily and she resented that. Now that he was gone, there would be no opportunity for her to have a meaningful relationship with her grandfather.

People are helped most by talking with a friend or relative about their loss. The same applies to children. Emily could have profited had she been able to explore her feelings with either of her parents. Her parents might also have profited because they may have developed a closer relationship with Emily and established a pattern of open communication.

As it was, Emily never did resolve the problem. Her parents suffered her sullenness without ever a clue as to what Emily was all about. Unfortunately, this lack of communication continued as Emily grew older and ever more a closed book.

John fared better. Harold recognized that John's nightmares were related to the loss. Harold made an effort to spend more time with the boy and not to be so critical when John acted up.

As for Peter, his parents tried to answer his questions as best as they were able. Elaine had the uneasy feeling that she was not answering them "the right way." She thought she made a mistake by saying that "Gramps is now at rest" because Peter asked if Gramps was sleeping. She thought that she might have caused Peter to confuse death and sleep.

Had Elaine investigated she could have found any number of excellent publications dealing with the subject. Many funeral homes provide families with complimentary pamphlets on how to answer children's questions about death. The local library and bookstore have any number of excellent publications designed to answer questions raised by small children.

Most religious organizations offer printed material for young people that explain death from the organization's perspective. For religious families, this is a good opportunity for the family to discuss their religious beliefs as they relate to the loss of a loved one.

INTERNET RESOURCES

Many Web sites offer free publications on how to deal with the issues of death and dying. You can use your browser to locate such sites.

Today's child is computer literate. A child may, on his own, decide to seek an E-mail buddy to work through a problem the child may be having with the death. Parents need to supervise such communication because the child may be especially vulnerable at this point in his/her life.

There are Web sites that offer organized E-mail grief support groups. One such site is GriefNet. This Web site is operated by Rivendell Resources, a non-profit organization:

GriefNet                                        (734) 761-1960
P.O. Box 3272
Ann Arbor, MI  48106-3272
          E-mail:   visibility@griefnet.org

KIDSAID is a companion Web site to GriefNet. They offer peer support groups for children who are dealing with a loss.   Parental permission is required before the child is allowed to join a support group.

    http://www.griefnet.org/KIDSAID/kids2kids.html

# THE TROUBLED CHILD

Most deaths are from natural causes. The death is expected and not all that difficult for the family to finally accept. The ***problem death*** is one that is tragic, unexpected, and/or a death that cuts short a life. More and more school officials are recognizing that the loss of a member of the school community deeply affects the student population. Many schools have adopted a policy of having school psychologists counsel the students as soon as the death occurs. They do not wait until a school child shows signs of being disturbed by the event.

It would be well for parents to adopt the same policy. Specifically, if your family suffers a problem death then consider seeking the services of a professional who is experienced in grief counseling just as soon after the death as is practicable.

A death does not always need to be a problem death to cause a problem in a child. As discussed before, if a child has unresolved issues, then that child may need professional assistance in coping with the loss. Children do not manifest grief or depression in the same way as adults, so look for changes that are atypical of the child and that do not resolve themselves within a reasonable time after the death. Consider consulting with a child psychologist if your child exhibits unusual or antisocial behavior such as:

- eating too much or too little
- destructive or aggressive behavior
- sleeping too much or too little
- misbehaving at school
- a sudden change in school performance

The red flag, signaling an immediate need for counseling, is a child who talks or writes about committing suicide. It is important to act quickly to show the child that you understand that he/she is having a rough time and that you and the doctor are going to assist the child with the problem.

There are any number of resources in the community to assist the child, from school counselors to religious organizations. The ILLINOIS PSYCHOLOGICAL ASSOCIATION, located in Chicago, offers a free referral service for all counties of the state. You can reach them at (312) 372-7610.

For those who cannot afford private care, counties offer low-cost services on an ability to pay basis. Some religious organizations offer counseling services to their members, as well as to the general public, on a sliding scale basis.

Before seeking counseling services, it is important to schedule a physical checkup for the child. There is a chance that the problem is physiological. Some illnesses cause behavioral changes; for example, food allergies can cause aggressive behavior. Hearing or visual deficiencies can cause a child to withdraw into himself. Even infections can cause behavioral disturbances. Perhaps the child is on drugs and an examination should pick that up. All these things need to be ruled out prior to counseling.

If your child has been treated by the physician over the years, the doctor may know the child well enough to be able to offer some insight into the problem. If the checkup does not reveal a physical problem, the physician may be able to suggest the right type of treatment, i.e., psychologist or psychiatrist, and perhaps give you a referral.

# CHOOSING THE RIGHT COUNSELOR

There was a film called GOOD WILL HUNTING in which a brilliant, but troubled, teenager was required, by court order, to attend counseling. The funniest part of the film was the manner in which the boy went through counselors. He deliberately alienated (and was alienated) by many doctors until he met the right one for him. Similarly, if your child needs counseling you might need to interview several counselors before you find someone with whom your child can work; someone who speaks on his/her level — someone the child can trust.

The issue of trust may create a dilemma for the parent. The child is the counselor's patient. The counselor cannot betray the child's trust by revealing what was said during treatment, yet parents need to know whether the treatment is helping the child. The counselor can, and should, disclose to the parent the diagnosis, prognosis and type of proposed treatment. The parents need to employ someone they trust to pursue the course of treatment that they determine is best for their child.

In seeking a counselor, personal references are the best avenue, although it may be difficult to find a friend or relation who has had his/her child successfully treated for a similar problem. With or without references, you need to investigate the counselor's background. What is his/her training? What percentage of the practice is devoted to children in this age group? Is the counselor experienced in working with children who are having difficulty coping with the loss of a loved one?

Interview more than one counselor before making your choice. If the child is sufficiently mature and able to cooperate in choosing the right counselor, then that is an important step forward. If not, you may need to be assertive and go with the counselor whom you trust and are most comfortable. If it turns out that there is no improvement within a few months, then you need to find another counselor. As with the student in GOOD WILL HUNTING, it may take several tries before you come upon someone who can help your child.

# STRATEGIES TO COPE WITH THE LOSS

Once the person accepts the fact of death, they are past the initial phase of the grief process. Most people do very well and are able to go through the remaining stages with no overt effort on their part. Others suffer profoundly and need to find ways to get through the grieving process. If you have recently experienced a loss and are having difficulty coping with the loss then consider your own personality type and explore those strategies that might help you through.

Do you enjoy socializing with people or do you prefer solitary activities? Are you a "do-it-yourself" type of person or do you feel more at ease with someone leading you through the process?

## STRATEGIES FOR THE PRIVATE PERSON

If you find socializing to be difficult, then consider non-social activities such as reading a self help book. There are many excellent publications that explore the grieving process and how to adjust to the loss. Praying or quiet meditation may offer you consolation. This may be a good time to explore different kinds of meditative techniques. You can find books on meditative techniques such as Zen or visualization in the Philosophy section of the library or bookstore. You can find books on Yoga in the exercise section.

If you are computer literate, then you can use your browser to locate an Internet support group. An anonymous friend may be the perfect confidant to help you to work through the sadness and loneliness that you are feeling. You can locate E-mail support groups for people who are dealing with all types of grief issues by searching the following topics: GRIEF    MOURNING    DEATH    DYING

# STRATEGIES FOR THE SOCIAL MINDED

If you are a social person, then consider using those types of activities that involve a social setting, such as joining a bridge, bowling or golfing group. If your grief is too deep to concentrate on recreational activities, consider joining a support group. The power of the support group is companionship. They offer the one thing you may need most at this time — just someone to listen.

If you belong to an organized religion or a civic organization, find out whether they have a support group for people who are going through a grieving process. If your organization does not have a support group, then consider starting one yourself. It can be as simple as putting a notice in a weekly bulletin that you are holding a meeting for anyone who lost a loved one within the past year. You can hold the meeting as part of a picnic or barbecue with everyone bringing a dish for others to share. Just getting together and sharing experiences may help you and others in your organization as well.

If you do not belong to an organization, then look in the newspaper for notices of meetings of local support groups or consider joining one of the many national support groups. The following are some of the well established national groups:

# FOR WIDOWED PERSONS

THEOS                             (412) 471-7779
(They Help Each Other Spiritually)
322 Boulevard of the Allies, Suite 105
Pittsburgh, PA   15222-1919

THEOS is a national organization with a volunteer network of recently widowed persons. They have support chapters in many states. If you wish to establish a support group in your area, they will help you to do so.

฿฿฿฿฿฿฿฿฿฿฿฿฿฿฿฿฿฿฿฿฿฿฿฿฿฿฿฿฿฿฿฿฿฿

AARP GRIEF AND LOSS PROGRAM
WIDOWED PERSONS SERVICE          (800) 424-3410
601 E Street NW
Washington, DC  20049

AARP has support groups for widowed persons throughout the United States. They also have support groups for adults who have suffered the loss of a family member such as a parent or sibling. You can call the above 800 number and they will let you know if there is a support group in your area.

 E-mail: griefandloss@ aarp.org
Web site: www.aarp.org/griefprograms

## FOR WIDOWED PARENTS

PARENTS WITHOUT PARTNERS    (800)637-7974
401 N. Michigan Avenue
Chicago, IL   60611-6267

PARENTS WITHOUT PARTNERS is a national non-profit organization for single parents. They offer group discussions and single parent activities such as picnics and hikes. They have some 9 chapters in the state of Illinois. Their national headquarters in Illinois can direct you to the chapter nearest you.

E-mail: pwp@sba.com
Web Site: http://parentswithoutpartners.org

## PET GRIEF SUPPORT SERVICES

Those who suffer the loss of a pet may experience a sense of loss similar to the loss of a close family member. Often they hesitate to turn to friends or family members (especially those who never owned a pet) believing they just wouldn't understand.

Some local Humane Societies provide a pet loss counseling service. The Lincolnshire Animal Hospital has a volunteer pet counselor who can be reached at (847) 634-9250.

There is a list of pet grief counseling services for other states at
http://www.superdog.com/

# BE GOOD TO YOU

People who suffer extreme grief tend to become extreme in everyday activities. They may forget to eat. Some find themselves eating all day. Some mourners develop sleep disturbances and go without sleep for long periods of time while others suffer the opposite extreme of wanting to sleep all day. If you find that your grief is affecting your physical well being, then you need to make a conscious effort to care for yourself:

## ✴ EAT A BALANCED NUTRITIONAL DIET

Contrary to popular taste, sugar, salt, fat and chocolate do not constitute the four basic food groups. And contrary to current food faddism, no one diet fits all. The ability to digest certain foods varies from person to person and we all have ethnic preferences. You need to learn what balance of fats, protein (meat, fish, legumes) and carbohydrates (fruit, vegetables, grains) you require to maintain your optimum weight and state of well being; and then make an effort to keep that balance in your daily diet.

## ✴ GET SUFFICIENT REST

There is much variation in the amount of sleep required from person to person. You know how much sleep you normally require. Try to maintain your usual, pre-loss, sleep pattern. If you are finding difficulty sleeping at night, resist the urge to sleep during the day. It is easy to reverse your days and nights. Awake all night, dozing all day, will only make you feel as if you are walking around in a fog.

## ✭ EXERCISE EACH DAY

Exercise can be as simple as taking a brisk 20 minute walk, however the more sustained and energetic, the greater the benefit. If you are having trouble sleeping at night, try exercising during the late afternoon and eating your main meal at lunch rather than late at night.

## ✭ THINK POSITIVE THOUGHTS

Make an effort to concentrate on things in your life that are right, as opposed to thoughts that make you angry or sad. This may be difficult to do. During periods of high stress, you may feel as if your mind has a mind of its own. Thoughts may race through your mind even though you'd just as soon not think them. Prayer and/or meditation may help you to reestablish discipline in your thinking process.

Eating right, getting sufficient sleep, exercising and thinking positive thoughts — most people have heard these recommendations from so many sources (doctors, psychologists, writers for health magazines, etc.) that they seem to have become a cliche. But the reason that so many professionals make these suggestions is simply that they work. Doing all these things will make you feel significantly better.

But if you feel so down that you are unable to help yourself, then you may need professional help to get you through this difficult period. Check with your health care plan to see if they will cover the cost of a visit to a psychiatrist or psychologist.

# ADJUSTING TO A NEW LIFE STYLE

If you lost a member of your immediate family, then in addition to going through the stages of the grieving process, you need to go through a transition period in which you learn how to live without the decedent. The child must learn to live without the guidance of a parent. Parents may need to put their parenting behind them. The spouse must learn to live without a partner, and as a single person.

In addition to learning to live with the loss, the bereaved may need to establish a new identity. Such was the case with Claire. She and Fred were married 44 years when he died after a lengthy battle with cancer. At first Claire didn't think she could live without him. She had been a wife for so long. She had trouble thinking of herself as a single person — nonetheless being one.

Claire had difficulty accepting the fact that Fred was dead, even though she expected he would die for months before he did. She would see Fred in her dreams. Sometimes she thought she saw him sitting in his favorite chair. When Fred appeared to Claire, he looked the same as when they were first married. Sometimes she thought he was speaking to her.

What was most comforting to Claire was that Fred was smiling at her. She was relieved to know that Fred was no longer in pain and was at peace. The smile on his face was a relief to her because she feared he might be angry with her for the many times he would call out her name and she would become annoyed with him. She felt guilty that she did not have more patience as a caregiver.

Claire found herself talking to Fred especially during those times that she was undecided as to what to do. As time progressed, she began to incorporate her husband's beliefs into her own so that instead of asking herself "What should I do?" it became "This is what Fred would have done."

Eventually Claire found that she was able to function on her own. She began to re-engage with the world. She found new interests to pleasantly occupy her time. She learned how to live as a single person. She is now more self sufficient than at any other time in her life. She laments that Fred no longer visits her. She still misses him.

Claire was able to get beyond the grief. She did it on her own, though she will tell you that she did it with Fred's help.

Claire's case is not unusual. As verified by the AARP survey, most people adjust to the loss on their own, requiring only an assist from family and friends, but there is a percentage of the grieving population that will require assistance and need to seek professional grief counseling.

For those experiencing psychological problems prior to the death, the event of the death may be the precipitating factor to mental illness requiring treatment. Similarly, if a person had a drinking problem or a drug addiction before the death, the event of the death may exacerbate the addiction.

Some deaths are so violent or tragic, that even the sturdiest may be unable to resume their life without professional assistance. In the next section, we discuss ways of coping with the problem death.

# THE PROBLEM DEATH

As discussed, the problem death is one that is unexpected, tragic or a death that cuts short a life. Such a death is an immediate problem in terms of the funeral, burial and estate settlement, but the most difficult problem is getting through the mourning period.

The death of a child is always a problem death. Even if the child is an adult, the parent experiences extreme grief. No one expects to outlive his or her child. In these days of a lengthening life cycle, more and more parents may come to experience such a loss. The loss may come at a time when the parent is frail or in poor health, making it all the more difficult to deal with the loss.

The only thing harder than losing an adult child is losing a young child. Nothing compares to the intensity of grief experienced by a parent when a little one dies. Some parents believe they are losing their mind. Many feel that their lives can never have meaning again. Guilt and recrimination flow, "Maybe I could have prevented it." There is even guilt for returning to ordinary living. If the parents find themselves smiling, laughing or making love they think, "How can we be doing this? How can we ever be normal again?"

The family who experiences a tragic or violent death should consider seeking professional grief counseling as soon as practicable after the death. The grief counseling can be in the format of a self-help group. Participants are able to talk and share their pain with others like themselves who understand what they are experiencing.

There are many specialized self-help groups that provide literature and peer support for families who experience a problem death.

---

## FOR PRENATAL OR NEONATAL DEATHS

M.E.N.D. **M**ommies **E**nduring **N**eonatal **D**eath
P.O. Box 1007                                    (888)-695-MEND
Coppell, TX   75019

MEND provides monthly newsletters and has a web site that with information:.

http://www.mend.org
E-mail  rebekah@mend.org

☙☙☙☙☙☙☙☙☙☙☙☙☙☙☙☙☙☙☙☙☙☙☙☙☙☙☙☙☙☙☙☙

SHARE                                    (800) 821-6819
National Share Pregnancy and Infant Loss Support
St. Joseph Health Center
300 First Corporate Drive
St. Charles, MO   63012-2893

SHARE  is a resource center for bereaved parents.  They have support groups throughout the United States. You can call the national office for the telephone number of the support group in your state.

http://www.nationalshareoffice.com
E-mail  share@nationalshareoffice

## FOR FAMILIES OF A DECEASED CHILD

THE COMPASSIONATE FRIENDS
National Chapter: (630) 990-0010
P.O. Box 3696, Oak Brook, IL  60522
THE COMPASSIONATE FRIENDS have local chapters with volunteers (themselves bereaved parents) to accept telephone calls.

http://www.compassionatefriends.org
E-mail  tcf_national@prodigy.com

A.G.A.S.T (888) 774-7437
**A**LLIANCE OF **G**RANDPARENTS **A S**UPPORT IN **T**RAGEDY
P.O. Box 17281
Phoenix, AZ  85011-0281
AGAST supports grandparents, who have suffered the loss of a grandchild, with informational packets, peer contact and newsletters.

E-mail: GRANMASIDS@AOL.COM

SIDS ALLIANCE (800) 221-7437
SUDDEN INFANT DEATH SYNDROME ALLIANCE
1314 Bedford Avenue, Suite 210
Baltimore, MD   21208

The SIDS Alliance is a national, not-for-profit, voluntary organization.  Their web site offers information and the names and E-mail addresses of chapters in all of the states.

http//www.sidsalliance.org
E-mail: sids@ais.net

## FOR FAMILIES OF MURDERED CHILDREN

THE NATIONAL ORGANIZATION OF       (888) 818-POMC
PARENTS OF MURDERED CHILDREN, INC.
National Chapter
100 East Eighth Street, B-41
Cincinnati, OH    45202

POMC has support groups and contact people in each of the fifty states. There are five support groups in the state of Florida.  Contact the National Chapter for the group nearest you.

          http://www.pomc.com
          E-mail  natlpomc@aol.com

## FOR FAMILIES OF SUICIDES

AMERICAN ASSOCIATION OF SUICIDOLOGY  (202) 237-2280
4201 Connecticut Ave. NW, Suite 408
Washington, DC   20008

The American Association of Suicidology is a not-for-profit organization that promotes education, public awareness and research for suicide prevention. It serves as a national clearinghouse for information on suicide. You can call for the number of a support group nearest you.  Their web site has the names addresses and phone number of several organizations that offer counseling for families who have lost a loved one to suicide.

          http://www.suicidology.org

# BUT WHAT IF I CAN'T STOP GRIEVING?

We observed that there are five stages of grieving:
shock/disbelief,
anger/guilt
searching/pining
sadness/depression
acceptance of the loss.

There is no right way to grieve. You may pass through a stage rapidly or even skip a stage. You may get hung up in one of the stages and have difficulty getting beyond that emotion. Some psychologists refer to this as "stuckness." It's something like what happened to 45-rpm phonograph records that were popular in the 1940's and 1950's.

For the benefit of the digital generation who have no experience with phonographs, the record was played by means of a needle that glided over groves of a revolving disk (the record). Sometimes the needle would get stuck in a groove and play the same sound over and over again until the annoyed listener bumped it into the next groove.

If you are stuck in one of the stages of mourning you may think the suggestions in this section to be useless in your situation because they encourage you to be proactive, i.e., to actively seek to help yourself. If you are thinking:
"I **can't** help myself. " or
"If I could help myself, I wouldn't have this problem," then the first thing you need to understand, and accept, is that you have no other choice but to help yourself. The pain exists within you and nowhere else. Because the pain is internal and unique to you, only you can ease that pain. This does not mean that no one can help you to deal with the pain. It just means that you need to be interactive with the healing process; and in particular, you need to take the first step.

What is that first step? To answer that question you need to identify those areas of your life with which you are having difficulty. It might help to make a list of all of the things that are bothering you. Once you compose the list, look at the last item on the list. If you are like most people, you will initially avoid thinking about what is really troubling you. It may take the last item on the list for you to admit to yourself what is really causing the problem.

Once you identify the problem, the identification itself should suggest the solution. For example, suppose you find the holidays unbearable, then a solution may be to change your holiday routine. Instead of wearing yourself out shopping for gifts, use the money to treat yourself to a boat cruise. Tell everyone that this year you are taking a holiday from the holidays. You may find that people are just as tired of exchanging gifts as you are and that they gladly welcome the change.

If your problem is being lonely, then your solution will involve companionship. How you attain that companionship will depend on your personality. If you are lonely, but not a social person, consider adopting a pet. If you are civic minded, then you may find companionship as a volunteer for community activities. If you are physically active, then perhaps you can take up a new sport or even pick up a sport that you used to enjoy at an earlier time in your life. If you enjoy sports but are not in the best shape, perhaps you can coach children's team sports.

If your problem is that you are severely depressed, then the solution will involve medical and/or psychological methods of lifting the depression. If you decide to ask for medical assistance, you need to continue to be interactive. You cannot stand passively by saying "Now heal me." Pharmaceutical hyperbole notwithstanding, there is no magic pill. An antidepressant may help you to gain control of yourself, but you still need to work through the grief.

If you feel that you have tried it all and you still are unable to find peace and contentment in your life, then you need to ask the hard question:

"What is it about mourning that I really enjoy?" Strange question? Not really.

You may enjoy thinking of your loved one even if the thought gives you as much pain as pleasure. You may think that if you stop mourning then you truly lose the decedent. If that's the case, then compartmentalize your grief, that is, set aside a special time of the day to actively think about and/or grieve for your loved one and the rest of the day not to grieve or even think about the decedent.

Actively plan the grieving compartment of your day. You may wish to have a grieving routine, perhaps visit the grave site once a week; or quietly spend 15 minutes a day looking at pictures of the decedent or writing down your memories of the happy times you had together. If you have been discussing your grief with family or friends, restrict such talks to specific times, perhaps on the decedent's birthday, or on the anniversary of his death.

Set aside as much time each day as you believe you need to mourn, but here is the hard part — you need to exercise self restraint not to mourn, nor talk about, nor even think of the decedent during any other part of the day. If your mind wanders back to the sadness and loneliness of the loss, postpone it. Say to yourself, "Hold that thought till my next grieving compartment."

If you are speaking to someone, do not mention the decedent or how you are feeling about the loss until your scheduled grieving talk with that person. If the subject comes up during a conversation, then change the subject by saying "We'll talk about that later."

Hopefully you will find the pain of your loss to lessen over time, in frequency and/or intensity.

It isn't so much that time heals; it is more that you learn to heal yourself over time.

# Glossary

ADMINISTRATION The *administration* of a Probate Estate is the management and settlement of the decedent's affairs. There are different types of administration. See *Ancillary Administration, Summary administration* and *Supervised Administration.*

AFFIANT   An *affiant* is someone who signs an affidavit and swears that it is true in the presence of a Notary Public or person with authority to administer an oath.

AFFIDAVIT   An *affidavit* is a written statement of fact made by someone voluntarily and under oath, in the presence of a notary public or someone who has authority to administer an oath.

AGENT   An *agent* is someone who is authorized by another (the principal) to act for or in place of the principal.

ANATOMICAL GIFT   An *anatomical gift* is the donation of all or part of the body of the decedent for a specified purpose, such as transplantation or research.

ANCILLARY ADMINISTRATION An *ancillary administration* is a probate procedure that aids or assists the original (primary) probate proceeding. Ancillary administration is conducted in another state to determine the beneficiary of the decedent's property located within that state.

ANNUITANT   An *annuitant* is someone who is entitled to receive payments under an annuity contract.

ANNUITY An *annuity* is the right to receive periodic payments (monthly, quarterly) either for life or for a number of years.

ASSET  An *asset* is anything owned by someone that has a value, including personal property (jewelry, paintings, securities, cash, motor vehicles, etc.) and real property (condominiums, vacant lots, acreage, residences, etc.)

ATTESTING WITNESS: An *attesting witness* to a Will is someone who signs the Will, at the request of the person making the Will, for the purpose of proving that the will is valid, i.e., that the person who made the Will did sign it, and did so on his own free will.

BENEFICIARY  A *beneficiary* is one who benefits from the acts of another person. In this book, we refer to a beneficiary as one who inherits a gift from the decedent.

CLAIM  A *claim* against the decedent's estate is a demand for payment.  To be effective, the claim must be filed with the Probate court within the time limits set by law.

CODICIL  A *codicil* to a Will is an addition to a Will that changes certain parts of the Will.

COLUMBARIUM  A *columbarium* is a vault with niches (spaces) for urns that contain the ashes of cremated bodies.

COMMON LAW MARRIAGE  A *common law marriage* is one that is entered into without a state marriage license nor any kind of official marriage ceremony. A common law marriage is created by an agreement to marry, followed by the two living together as man and wife. Most states do not recognize a common law marriage as being a valid marriage.

CREMAINS  The word *cremains* is an abbreviation of the term *cremated remains*. It is also referred to as the *ashes* of a person who has been cremated.

**DECEDENT** The *decedent* is the person who died.

**DECEDENT'S REPRESENTATIVE** The *Decedent's Representative* is someone (the Administrator or Executor) appointed by the Probate court to settle the decedent's estate and to distribute whatever is left to the proper beneficiary.

**DEVISE** A *devise* is a gift of real property (land, condominium, etc.) made by means of a Will.

**DISTRIBUTION** The *distribution* of a trust estate or of a Probate Estate is the giving to the beneficiary that part of the estate to which the beneficiary is entitled.

**ESTATE** A person's *estate* is all of the property (both real and personal property) owned by that person.   A person's estate is also referred to as his *taxable estate* because all of the decedent's assets must be included when determining whether any Estate taxes are due when the person dies.   Compare to *Probate Estate*.

**FIDUCIARY** A *fiduciary* is one who holds property in trust for another or one who acts for the benefit of another.

**GRANTEE** The *grantee* of a deed (also called the party of the second part) named in a deed is the person who receives title to the property from the grantor.

**GRANTOR** A *grantor* is someone who transfers property. The grantor of a deed, is the person who transfers property to a new owner (the *grantee*). The grantor of a trust is someone who creates the trust and then transfers property into the trust.   Also see *settlor* and *trustor*.

HEALTH CARE AGENT   A *Health Care Agent* is a person appointed by someone (the principal) under a Health Care Power of Attorney to make health care decisions for the Principal in the event that the Principal is too ill to speak for himself.

HEALTH CARE DIRECTIVE A *Health Care Directive* is a statement made by someone (the principal) in the presence of witnesses or a written, notarized statement in which the principal gives directions about the care he/she wishes to receive. See *Living Will* and *Power of Attorney for Health Care*.

HEIR   An *heir* is someone who is entitled to inherit the decedent's property in the event that the decedent dies intestate (without a Will). This includes the surviving spouse and the state of Illinois, if the decedent had no surviving relative.

HOMESTEAD   The *homestead* is the dwelling and land owned and occupied in the state of Illinois as the owner's principal residence.

INDEPENDENT ADMINISTRATION
An *Independent Administration* is a probate procedure that is conducted with minimal court supervision.

INDIGENT   A person who is *indigent* is one who is poor, destitute and without funds.

INTESTATE   *Intestate* means not having a Will or dying without a Will. *Testate* is to have a Will or dying with a Will.

**IRREVOCABLE CONTRACT** An *irrevocable contract* is a contract that cannot be revoked, withdrawn, or cancelled by any of the parties to that contract.

**KEY MAN INSURANCE** *Key man insurance* is an insurance policy designed to protect a company from economic loss in the event that an important employee of the company becomes disabled or dies.

**LEGALESE** *Legalese* is the special vocabulary used by attorneys to draft legal documents. Many consider legalese to be unnecessarily complex and incomprehensible.

**LETTERS OF ADMINISTRATION** *Letters of Administration* is a document, issued by the Probate court, giving the person who is appointed as Administrator, authority to take possession of and to administer the estate of the decedent.

**LETTERS TESTAMENTARY** *Letters Testamentary* is a document given to the person who is the Executor of the decedent's Will that gives the Executor authority to take possession of and to administer the estate of the decedent.

**LIFE ESTATE** A *life estate* interest in real property is the right to possess and occupy that property for so long as the holder of the life estate lives.

**LINEAL DESCENDANT** A *lineal descendant* of the decedent is someone who is his direct descendant, such as his child, grandchild, great-grandchild etc.

**LITIGATION** *Litigation* is the process of carrying on a lawsuit, i.e., to sue for some right or remedy in a court of law.

LIVING WILL  A *Living Will* is a Health Care Directive that gives instructions about whether life support systems should be applied in the event that the person who signs the Living Will is terminally ill and unable to speak for himself.

MEDICAID  *Medicaid* is a public assistance program sponsored jointly by the federal and state government to provide medical care for people with low income.

NEXT OF KIN  *Next of kin* has two meanings in law: *next of kin* can refer to a person's nearest blood relation or it can refer to those people (not necessarily blood relations) who are entitled to inherit the property of the decedent if the decedent died without a will.

PERJURY  *Perjury* is lying under oath. The false statement can be made as a witness in court or by signing an Affidavit. Perjury is a criminal offense.

PERSONAL PROPERTY  *Personal property* is all property owned by a person that is not real property (real estate). It includes cars, stocks, house furnishings, jewelry, etc. Personal property is sometimes called *personalty*.

PER STIRPES GIFT  A *per stirpes* gift is a gift which is given to a group of people such that if one of them dies before the gift is given, then that deceased person's share goes to his/her lineal descendants.

POWER OF ATTORNEY  A *Power of Attorney* is a document that appoints an Agent to act for or on behalf of the person who signs the document (the Principal). The Power of Attorney states those things that the Agent can do on behalf of his Principal.

**POWER OF ATTORNEY FOR HEALTH CARE**  A *Power of Attorney for Health Care* is a document in which a person (the "Principal") appoints someone (his "Agent") to make medical decisions on behalf of the Principal in the event that the Principal is too ill to speak for himself.

**PRE-NUPTIAL AGREEMENT**  A *pre-nuptial agreement* (also known as an *antenuptial agreement*) is an agreement made prior to marriage whereby a couple determines how their property is to be managed during their marriage and how their property is to be divided should one die, or they later divorce.

**PROBATE**  *Probate* is a court procedure in which a court determines the existence of a valid Will and then supervises the distribution of the Probate Estate of the decedent.

**PROBATE ESTATE**  The *Probate Estate* is that part of the decedent's estate that is subject to probate.  It includes property that the decedent owned in his name only.  It does not include property that was jointly held by the decedent and someone else.  It does not include property held "in trust for" or "for the benefit of" someone.

**REAL PROPERTY**  *Real property,* also known as *real estate,* is land and anything permanently attached to the land such as buildings and fences.

**REPARATION**  *Reparation* is money paid to make up for an injury or wrongdoing

RESIDUARY BENEFICIARY  A *residuary beneficiary* is a beneficiary named in a Will who is to receive all or part of whatever is left of the Probate Estate once the specific gifts made in the Will have been distributed and once the decedent's bills, taxes and costs of probate have been paid.

RESIDUARY ESTATE A *residuary estate* is that part of a probate estate that is left after all expenses and costs of administration have been paid and specific gifts have been distributed.

SETTLOR  A *settlor* is someone who furnishes property that is placed in a trust.   If the settlor is also the creator of the trust, then the settlor is also referred to as the grantor or trustor.

SPENDTHRIFT TRUST  A *Spendthrift Trust* is a trust created to provide monies for the living expenses of a beneficiary, and at the same time protect the monies from being taken by the creditors of the beneficiary.

STATUTE OF LIMITATION   A *statute of limitation* is a federal or state law that sets maximum time periods for taking legal action. Once the time set out in the statute passes, no legal action can be taken.

SUMMARY ADMINISTRATION  *Summary Administration* is a short, simple probate procedure designed to settle small estates.

SUPERVISED ADMINISTRATION  *A Supervised Administration* is a probate procedure in which the Decedent's Representative is required to seek court approval before taking certain actions.

SURETY ON A BOND   The *surety on a bond* for probate procedures is usually an insurance company who will guarantee to pay the beneficiaries of the estate any loss they suffer as a result of the failure of the Decedent's Representative to do his job properly.

TENANCY BY THE ENTIRETY   A *Tenancy by the Entirety* is the same as a Joint Tenancy with rights of survivorship, modified by the common-law theory that a husband and wife are one person.

TENANCY IN COMMON   *Tenancy in common* is a form of ownership such that each tenant owns his/her share without any claim to that share by the other tenants. Unlike a joint tenancy, there is no right of survivorship. Once a tenant in common dies, his/her share belongs to the tenant's estate and not to the remaining owners of the property.

TESTATE   *Testate* means having a Will or dying with a Will.

TITLE INSURANCE   *Title Insurance* is a policy issued by a title company after searching title to the property. The policy insures the accuracy of its search against any claim of a defective title.

TRUST AGREEMENT   A *trust agreement* is document in which someone (the Grantor or Trustor) creates a trust and appoints a trustee to manage property placed into the trust. The usual purpose of the trust is to benefit persons or charities named by the Grantor as beneficiaries of the trust.

TRUSTEE   A *trustee* is a person, or institution, who accepts the duty of caring for property for the benefit of another.

TRUSTOR   The *Trustor* is the creator of a trust.

UNDUE INFLUENCE   *Undue influence* is pressure or persuasion that overpowers a person's free will so that the dominated person is not acting intelligently or voluntarily.

WAIVER   A *waiver* is the intentional and voluntary giving up of a known right.

WARRANTY DEED   A *warranty deed* is a deed in which someone (the Grantor) transfers the property to another (the Grantee) and guarantees good title, i.e., the Grantor guarantees that he has the right to transfer the property, and that no one else has any right to the property.

# INDEX

## A

# S

# T

# U

UNCLAIMED PROP.                   64, 65

UNIFORM GIFT TO MINOR ACT
                                  182, 190

UNIFIED TAX EXCLUSION
                            36,178, 180

# V

VETERANS
  Administration                  17,18
  Burial                        17, 149
  Indigent                          19
  National Cemetery            16, 149
  Spouse                       17, 149

VIOLENT DEATH                       20

# W

WEB SITES
  AARP                            239
  AGAST                           247
  Amer. Assoc. Suicid.            248
  American Bar Assoc.              xv
  Compassionate Friends           247
  Dept. of Labor (Federal)         48
  Eagle Pub. Co.               43, 65
  GriefNet                        232
  Illinois Abandoned Prop.         64
  Illinois Dept. of Insur.        202
  Illinois Statutes                xi
  IRS                             129
  Medicare                         47
  MEND                            246

WEB SITES (continued)
  Office Person. Mgmt              30
  Parents W/O Partners            240
  Pet Support                     240
  POMC                            248
  SHARE                           246
  SIDS Foundation                 247
  Social Security Admin.           28
  THEOS                           239
  Veteran's Admin.                 17

WILL
  Challenging                     113
  Deposit with court               67
  Foreign                          67
  Holographic                     114
  Locating                         67
  Missing will                     69
  Out of state                     67
  Preparing a Will           183, 184
  Problem Will                    114

# BOOK ORDER

MAIL ORDER:  EAGLE PUBLISHING COMPANY OF BOCA
4199 N. DIXIE HWY. #2
BOCA RATON, FL 33431
INTERNET ORDER: www.eaglepublishing.com
FAX ORDER: (561) 338-0823     TELEPHONE ORDER (800) 824-0823

SHIP TO:  NAME _____

ADDRESS: _____

METHOD OF PAYMENT:     CHECK

☐ VISA     ☐ MASTER CARD     ☐ DISCOVER     ☐ AMER. EXP.

☐☐☐☐☐ ☐☐☐☐☐ ☐☐☐☐☐ ☐☐☐☐☐

**EXPIRATION DATE** _____

PAPER BACK $25   HARD COVER  $32
PRICE INCLUDES SHIPPING/HANDLING

| | QUANTITY | AMOUNT |
|---|---|---|
| When Someone Dies In Alabama | | |
| When Someone Dies In Arizona | | |
| When Someone Dies In California | | |
| When Someone Dies In Colorado | | |
| When Someone Dies In Florida | | |
| When Someone Dies In Georgia | | |
| When Someone Dies In Illinois | | |
| When Someone Dies in Louisiana | | |
| When Someone Dies In Maryland | | |
| When Someone Dies In Massachusetts | | |
| When Someone Dies In Michigan | | |
| When Someone Dies In Mississippi | | |
| When Someone Dies In New Jersey | | |
| When Someone Dies In New York | | |
| When Someone Dies In North Carolina | | |
| When Someone Dies In Ohio | | |
| When Someone Dies In Pennsylvania | | |
| When Someone Dies In Tennessee | | |
| When Someone Dies In Texas | | |
| When Someone Dies In Virginia | | |
| When Someone Dies In Washington | | |
| | **TOTAL** | |

It is the goal of EAGLE PUBLISHING COMPANY to keep our publications fresh.

As we receive information about changes to the federal or state law we will post an update to this edition at our Web site:
http://www.eaglepublishing.com

If you do not have Internet access, call us at (800) 824-0823
and we will mail the update to you.